W9-BUH-063

Easy Maintenance Gardening

Created and designed by the editorial staff of ORTHO BOOKS

Edited by   *Ken Burke*
Written by   *A. Cort Sinnes*
Designed by   *James Stockton*

Ortho Books

Publisher
Robert L. Iacopi

Editorial Director
Min S. Yee

Managing Editor
Anne Coolman

Horticultural Editor
Michael D. Smith

Senior Editor
Kenneth R. Burke

Production Manager
Laurie S. Blackman

Horticulturists
Michael D. McKinley
Deni W. Stein

Editors
Barbara J. Ferguson
Susan M. Lammers
Sally W. Smith

Production Assistants
Darcie S. Furlan
Julia W. Hall

National Sales Manager
Garry P. Wellman

Operations/Distribution
William T. Pletcher

Operations Assistant
Donna M. White

Administrative Assistant
Georgiann Wright

Address all inquiries to:
Ortho Books
Chevron Chemical Company
Consumer Products Division
575 Market Street
San Francisco, CA 94105

Copyright © 1982
Chevron Chemical Company
Printed in the United States of America
All rights reserved under international
and Pan-American copyright
conventions.

No portion of this book may be
reproduced without written permission
from the publisher.

Every effort has been made at the time
of publication to guarantee the
accuracy of the names and addresses
of information sources and suppliers
and in the technical data contained.
However, the reader should check for
his or her own assurance and must be
responsible for selection and use of
suppliers and supplies, plant materials
and chemical products.

We are not responsible for unsolicited
manuscripts, photographs, or
illustrations.

First Printing in August, 1982

1 2 3 4 5 6 7 8 9

82 83 84 85 86 87

ISBN 0-89721-004-2

Library of Congress Catalog Card
Number 82-82160

Chevron Chemical Company
575 Market Street, San Francisco, CA 94105

Front cover:
Michael McKinley
White oleanders, blue agapanthus,
and blue statice dominate this easy
maintenance garden and patio,
designed by Jack Chandler of St.
Helena, California.

Back cover:
Susan Lammers
Brick and stone provide a natural-
looking, low maintenance floor for this
San Francisco garden. Cyclamen in
pots lend seasonal color.

Title page:
Michael McKinley
This Kansas City garden was
designed by Michael McKinley to stay
green and refreshing throughout the
midwestern summer. Clockwise from
the left, plants include bayberry, white
pine, staghorn sumac, crabapple,
eulalia grass, prostrate juniper, and
fountain grass.

Consultants:
Jack Chandler and Associates, L.A.,
St. Helena, CA
Robert Chesnut, L.A., Charleston, SC
Barbara Fealy, L.A., Portland, OR
Carlton B. Lees, L.A.
Oehme, Van Sweden & Associates,
L.A., Washington, DC

Acknowledgments:
Andropogon Associates, L.A.,
Philadelphia, PA
The Arnold Arboretum, Jamaica
Plains, MA
Dr. Ernesta Ballard, Philadelphia, PA
David Benner, New Hope, PA
The Birmingham Botanic Garden,
Birmingham, AL
The Boerner Botanical Gardens of
Whitnall Park, Hales Corner, WI
F.H. Cabot, Cold Spring, NY
Richard Chisholm, San Francisco, CA
James David, L.A., Austin, TX
Roy Davidson, Seattle, WA
Harold Epstein, Larchmont, NY
Barry Ferguson Designs,
Oyster Bay, NY
H. Lincoln Foster, Falls Village, CN
Dan Franklin, L.A., Atlanta, GA
Christopher C. Friedrichs, L.A., New
Orleans, LA
Garden in the Woods,
Framingham, MA
Katherine Hull, Manchester, MA
Frederick and Mary Ann McGourty,
Norfolk, CN
Old Westbury Gardens, Westbury, NY
Panfield Nurseries, Cold Spring
Harbor, NY
Planting Fields Arboretum. Oyster
Bay, NY
Rosedown Gardens, Bellevue, WA
Strybing Arboretum, San
Francisco, CA
Ernest Wertheim, L.A., San
Francisco, CA
Jane Wilson Photo Research,
Hillsborough, CA

Typography by Vera Allen, Castro
Valley, CA
Color separations by Colorscan,
Mountain View, CA
Copy editing and additional writing by
Judy Chaiffin

Illustrations:
Cyndie Clark-Huegel, pages 28, 29,
31, 46, 47, 48, 50, 57, 60, 61, and 64.
Mark Pechenik, pages 13, 16, 18, 22,
and 27.

Photography:
Names of photographers in
alphabetical order are followed by
page numbers on which their work
appears. R = right, C = center, L =
left, T = top, B = bottom.
William C. Aplin: 83BR.
Josephine Coatsworth: 51R, 55, 74C.
Derek Fell: 74TR, 75TL, 76R, 77TL,
77TR, 79TR, 80TR, 81TL, 82TL, 82TR,
83TL, 83TR, 84TL, 84TR, 85TR, 86TL,
86BR, 87L, 88BC, 89TL, 89BC, 90TR,
92TL, 92TR, 92BL, 93TL, 93BR,
94BL.
Pamela Harper: 75TR, 75BL, 76C,
77BR, 78BL, 79TC, 80TL, 84BR,
85BL, 86TR, 86BL, 88TL, 88TC,
91TR, 91BL, 91BR.
Michael Landis: 18B, 19, 27, 32T,
33TL, 33CR, 51L, 81TR, 85TC.
Michael McKinley: 4, 5, 6, 7L, 7R, 8T,
8B, 9, 10, 11, 12T, 12L, 12R, 13, 14,
15, 16, 17T, 17B, 18T, 20, 21, 23TL,
23TR, 23B, 24, 25, 26, 30T, 30B, 32B,
33CL, 33BL, 33TR, 33BR, 35TL,
35TR, 35BL, 36, 37, 39, 41L, 41R,
42T, 42BL, 42BR, 43TL, 43TR, 43BL,
44, 49, 54, 58, 67, 71, 74TL, 74CL,
76L, 77BL, 78TL, 78R, 79TL, 79BC,
80BR, 82BR, 87R, 89TR, 90TL, 90CR,
91TL, 93TC, 93TR, 94TL, 94TR,
94BR.
James McNair: 86TC.
George Taloumis: 85BL.
Wolf von dem Bussche: 81BR.

Easy Maintenance Gardening

Gardens for Today's Gardeners

A garden that's both attractive and easy to maintain is the goal of many of today's busy gardeners. Here you'll find a step-by-step guide to meeting that goal, from planning, through planting, to sitting back, relaxing, and enjoying your creation.

Easy maintenance gardening is a popular subject. Mention the words *easy maintenance,* and a surprising number of gardeners will turn to you with attentive eyes and suddenly sensitive ears and the comment, "Now that's what I'd like to know more about." In our efforts to find out "more about" the subject, we learned that its scope was even wider than we had imagined. Our search was a long one with many stops along the way while we talked at length with gardeners, nursery and garden center personnel, maintenance professionals, and landscape architects and other designers. The broad scope of the information in this book is the result of what we heard from all the people involved in one aspect or another of gardening. We're pleased to announce that the story of easy maintenance has a happy ending. The concepts *easy maintenance* and *gardens* can go together quite successfully.

Easy maintenance gardens do indeed exist. These gardens are based on well-defined spaces and simple and effective designs, *planned* from the very beginning with the goal of easy maintenance in mind. They make good use of up-to-the-minute advances in technology, such as automatic watering systems, as well as time-honored practices of advance preparation without which no garden can ever be easy to maintain. Plants in these easy maintenance gardens are chosen not only for their appropriateness in terms of scale and proportion but also for their suitability to the climate. Newer varieties of familiar plant friends—

Left: Japanese gardens are considered good subjects for low maintenance interpretations. Here, Japanese maple, aucuba, and liriope combine in a protected side garden. Right: Clematis, leatherleaf mahonia, nandina, liriope, Chinese holly, and English ivy transform this shaded, narrow space into a usable outdoor room. Both gardens were designed by Atlanta Landscape Architect Dan Franklin.

those that are naturally compact, that have increased disease and pest resistance, and that are adaptable to a wider range of growing conditions—are always favored. If you supplement the ideas and technologies making up this broad framework by using the many tools specifically designed to lessen the work involved in common garden chores, what is the result? A garden that looks the way you want it to—and one that's easy to maintain.

We suggest in this book that you follow a number of different procedures that may at first appear to be unrelated to the goal of easy maintenance. For example, you may be surprised to find here detailed advice on how to prepare soil in advance for the planting of a lawn or ground cover and a step-by-step method for planting trees and shrubs. What does this hard, careful work have to do with easy maintenance? According to our consultants, the message is clear: You can't get something for nothing. Hard work now can mean easy work later, and it is in support of this truism that we have included the information we have about *all* the factors involved in the creation of an easy maintenance garden. This approach bypasses superficial solutions to maintenance problems, which seldom turn out to be solutions in the long run.

THOMAS CHURCH AND THE EASY MAINTENANCE GARDEN

During the early 1950s, several revolutionary architects redefined interior living spaces in response to how modern Americans indicated they wanted to live. Postwar economic conditions and changing ideas resulting from widespread GI experiences with other cultures had led people to have different expectations of their at-home surroundings than they had had before. Translated into architectural terms, this meant slab floors instead of basements and traditional raised foundations, "window walls," sliding glass doors (now commonplace, of course), and rooms less strictly defined structurally. The barriers between house and garden were dissolved in a "curtain of glass." The modern trend toward easy maintenance gardening grew directly out of this revolution in housing architecture.

Thomas Church (1902–1978), one of America's leading landscape architects, extended this innovative philosophy one step

farther. He took it into the garden: If the garden could become part of the house, the house could become part of the garden. In studying the new way his clients wanted to use their surrounding space, Church developed gardens unlike any that had been seen before. He placed the emphasis on outdoor living rather than on gardening: There were patios for sunbathing and relaxing; there were outdoor areas for cooking and eating; there were service areas for storing tools and for accommodating such everyday tasks as hanging out clothes to dry. Whether it was Church's conscious aim or not, these gardens embodied the principles of easy maintenance gardening.

Even though Church promoted gardens created for practical use as opposed to gardens contrived for the sake of beauty alone, Church's gardens were indeed beautiful. His knowledge and skill in using plants was second only to his ability as a designer. Not so

Thomas Church's own garden in San Francisco, California, as it looks today. Foreground: Agapanthus, bonsai pine, petunias, and geraniums in pots on landing under cherry tree. Midground: Boxwood hedge in freeform shape around roses. Tulips and petunias in pots. Background: Algerian ivy trained on wire wall, and palm.

with many who worked with his ideas. As you might imagine, there can be hazards in viewing plant material as mere decoration for outdoor living spaces. Plants are and always have been the basis of any self-respecting garden. When people less skilled and sensitive than Church interpreted some of Church's theories, the results were less than satisfactory from an aesthetic point of view. Some of Church's theories when taken to their logical extreme could, and frequently did, produce gardens with all the appeal and comfort of a parking lot.

There is now ample evidence to suggest that the oversimplification resulting in the parking lot effect—an uninviting and standardized approach to the home garden—is becoming a thing of the past. After years of ruthlessly subtracting elements from the garden for the sake of easier maintenance, many of today's gardeners are attempting to put a few of the niceties back in—and to do so without adding an unmanageable amount of maintenance to the scene. And that is what this book is all about.

HOW TO USE THIS BOOK

If you are committed to the idea of creating an attractive easy maintenance garden, this book bears reading in its entirety. You will be able to get a better grasp of the elements involved if you read the material from start to finish rather than sampling here and there. If special interests dictate, the following material will direct you to information subject by subject, as will the index.

Easy Maintenance by Design

There is no question that a garden designed from the beginning with respect for the goal of easy maintenance is the most successful at meeting that goal. Although it is usually easier to design such a garden from scratch than it is to redesign an already existing garden, any and all of the ideas presented throughout the book are applicable to both situations. Our interviews with the five landscape architects in the following chapter (beginning on page 11) established clearly the primary relationship between design and maintenance. Taken in total, the information in these interviews amounts to a home study course given by professionals who have made designing easy maintenance gardens their specialty. We think that you will find their comments very useful as you begin to think about ways to modify or create your own easy maintenance landscape.

For information on how to go about deciding what you need a garden to do for you, see pages 25–26. The list of questions there will help you to approach the problem from the standpoint of both intended use and resources. Considered simplicity is a key concept in coming up with a workable, satisfactory plan. Translating a design into a plan is discussed on pages 29–31. Thinking of a garden as an outdoor room, with walls, a floor, and a ceiling, is a useful device for design and planning. This approach to conceptualizing your garden is discussed on pages 31–38. Choices for floors, ceilings, and walls appear there.

Clear-cut design is the first step in making an easy maintenance garden. Left: This circle drive approach to the house at the rear was designed by Oehme, van Sweden & Associates of Washington, D.C., using sedum 'Autumn Joy', fountain grass, giant eulalia grass, calamagrostis grass, and yucca. Right: This narrow entrance walk is planted with boxwood, euonymus, and caladiums, mulched with bark.

Plant Selection

Without plants, a garden—easy maintenance or not—is simply not a garden. Once you have arrived at a design that at the same time makes good use of the garden space and provides for your special garden needs, you can begin to consider what you will plant. To help you in the process, a number of plants are described in the Plant Selection Guide, beginning on page 73. All are likely candidates for happiness in an easy maintenance garden. Plants are also listed, by category—trees, shrubs, ground covers, flowering plants, and so on—on pages 39–40. One object in choosing plants for a landscape is to create a willing garden, one in which plants grow well without a great deal of coaxing from the gardener. This means choosing plants that are well adapted to your climate, soil conditions, and the level of attention you are willing to give. In this connection, you might want to consider the merits of creating a modified natural landscape. This option is discussed on pages 41–43. The other object in plant selection is to choose plants that attract you. No matter how little care a plant needs, if you don't like it, you won't enjoy having it in your garden. Plant selection is discussed in one form or another throughout this book, but it receives special attention in connection with the discussion of elements in your plan, pages 31–38.

By limiting the diversity of plants used, the maintenance the garden requires can be significantly reduced. Here, the foreground is planted with box-wood and vinca major; in the background, citrus in tubs, pelargoniums, and a privet hedge.

Advance Preparation for Easy Maintenance

Taking the time to design and prepare a garden properly from the beginning will go a long way in helping you cut back on future maintenance chores. Work done at this initial stage of garden development (or redevelopment) will give you the greatest returns, and, for the most part, it is work that you have to do only once.

Even so, a quick glance at Chapter 4 (beginning on page 45) may cause you to think, "If this is easy maintenance, who needs it?" But a flower or shrub border that is planted without adequate soil preparation will always struggle along, making extra demands on the disappointed owner, in the same way that a lawn that is carelessly installed will always be more difficult to mow, water, and maintain than one planned with ease of maintenance in mind. Your aim, after all, is to develop a thriving, healthy garden that essentially grows as much by itself as possible.

If you're starting from scratch or planning a major overhaul of an existing garden, the information in Chapter 4 will be of particular interest to you. The techniques we cover range from technological innovations to helpful tips to fundamentals of gardening—past and present. No one can deny the benefits of adequate soil preparation for lawns and ground covers nor its ultimate influence on maintenance. The same holds true for following a time-honored procedure in planting trees and shrubs. One of the best methods we know of for lowering maintenance in the garden across a whole range of garden chores—watering, weeding, tending for general plant health—is mulching. For a restatement of an old garden practice, see the section on this subject, pages 52–55.

Edging is one of those things that few gardeners give much thought to, but carefully designed and installed edging may be

This Portland, Oregon garden features good use of bark mulch, 2-by-4 edging, a gravel walk, and a preponderance of broad-leafed evergreens. Clockwise from lower left, plants include white azaleas, tree peonies, dwarf cherry laurel, violets and pansies under snowball viburnum, camellia, rhododendron, scilla, ajuga, and rhododendron.

one of the reasons your neighbors have finished tending their lawn after fifteen minutes while you're still at it an hour later. For information on edgings in a variety of situations, see pages 47 and 48.

Although it's said that there is very little new on the subject of gardening, advances in watering techniques make the assertion questionable. New systems are available in varying degrees of sophistication that can all but eliminate the gardener's responsibility in meeting the garden's need for water, thus changing the entire concept of gardening. See pages 49–51.

Ongoing Chores

Many labor- and time-saving tools have gained popular acceptance—the power lawn mower, the nylon string trimmer, the electric hedge trimmer, push-type edgers, and the scuffle hoe, to mention just a few. Gardeners interested in reducing the amount of time they spend working in the garden will do well to consider how they might use to that end the many available power tools, hand tools (both old style and redesigned), and other innovative garden equipment. Chapter 5, beginning on page 59, describes several tools and types of equipment that can be of inestimable value in the easy maintenance garden. If you are creating a brand-new garden or thinking about redoing your present garden, you will want to ponder at some length the options presented there. There's no doubt that having the right equipment for any job goes a long way toward making the job easier.

The garden jobs homeowner dislike most, and hence put off the longest (making them into an even bigger job), are a matter of record. Weeding, raking and disposing of leaves, just about all phases of lawn care, and watering, especially in midsummer vacation time, are at the top of most people's list of dislikes. Pruning trees and shrubs remains such a mystery to most people that they don't even consider it a regular garden chore.

You may find yourself saying: "I don't really mind doing those jobs, I just don't like doing them so often, or for so many hours out of a short weekend." It is a point well taken. Many aversions to garden maintenance have to do with the size of the job rather than the job itself. Weeding a large, overgrown flower bed, planted in a state of spring exuberance, is a far different job than picking the weeds from a raised flower bed on the way to the mailbox. Keeping gardens down to a size that you feel comfortable with is one important consideration in keeping maintenance easy. Another is timing. "Take care of a job while it is still small" is an oft-repeated but seldom heeded bit of advice. To help you with your timing and perhaps to give you a boost out the door, be sure to read "A Seasonal Guide to Easy Maintenance," starting on page 69. Whatever the season, you'll find valuable, work-reducing information.

For taming some of the other all-time disliked garden jobs, refer to a specific subject, for example:

Weeding: See the section on mulching, pages 52–55; for other weed control techniques, see pages 63–65.

For some ideas on how to remove leaves from your yard, see page 68, and for ideas on how to keep them from becoming a problem in the first place, see page 39 for lists of evergreen shrubs and trees.

For help in all phases of watering—from lawns to containers—see pages 49–52 and pages 60–62.

For coming as close as you can to an easy maintenance lawn, see page 32 and pages 45–47.

And if pruning is a mystery to you, and likely to remain that way, see the list on page 39 for plants that need little or no pruning. Also see the information on pages 66 and 67 about pruning equipment.

LOOKING AHEAD

In our desire not to distort the picture, we have presented what we consider to be the whole easy maintenance story. If at first glance this approach seems overwhelming and the emphasis on design disproportionate, be advised that a garden that is truly easy maintenance is the result of following many seemingly disparate paths. We know that these paths converge in actual gardens. We have seen easy maintenance gardens, walked in them, and have talked to the owners, who have given us the details of their successes. In sharing this information with you, we hope to inspire you to start on the road to your own easy maintenance garden and to give you confidence that success commensurate with your efforts and desires can indeed be yours.

The Professional Approach

The four professional landscape architects we interviewed about easy maintenance had different ideas about a lot of things, but they all agreed on two points: the need for a strong, unifying design, and the importance of thorough soil preparation before you plant anything.

Left: This back patio garden was designed by New Orleans landscape architect Christopher Friedrichs. The trees are river birch. Dracaena in pots is echoed by yucca in the ground. The brick walk is edged with an English ivy ground cover. Right: Easy maintenance does not have to mean uninteresting gardens. In this California garden, Japanese maple, ferns, tree fern, star jasmine, and baby's-tears are planted together in a study of contrasting textures and harmony of color.

On the next eighteen pages, four landscape architects put forth their ideas on easy maintenance gardens: Jack Chandler, St. Helena, California; Robert Chesnut, Charleston, South Carolina; Barbara Fealy, Portland, Oregon; and Oehme, van Sweden & Associates, Washington, D.C..

These architects were chosen because they are interested in easy maintenance gardens and because their work uniquely reflects the regions in which they work. Some of what they have to say may surprise you, and some you might disagree with, but one point is clear: There is no one set of rules governing what is and what is not an easy maintenance garden.

As the photographs graphically illustrate, there is room for an admirable amount of diversity and beauty—all within the range of easy maintenance gardening. Simply taking the time to think and plan carefully for your garden, as these people are in the business of doing, will immeasurably enhance your garden results and pleasure.

Defining an outdoor space—boldly—is a cardinal rule in simplifying garden maintenance. It is also an important key to producing any attractive garden, easy maintenance or otherwise. A garden with uncertain boundaries—a creeping lawn area, plants placed willy-nilly without any relationship to one another, a dog run that doubles as a children's play area and is sometimes used to dry clothes—can sabotage a gardener's best intentions. The overwhelming question becomes: "Where do I start?"

Jack Chandler,
St. Helena, California

Jack Chandler is a landscape architect whose work is spread out over the wide open spaces of the Southwest and California. His bold, geometric designs distinctly show the human hand on the landscape without an artificial formality that runs counter to natural harmony. His gardens are pleasing gardens, both large and small, revealing an artist's regard for the juxtaposition of form, line, color, and texture. Chandler's landscapes are made to be lived in, played on, and entertained around, but above all, they are easy to maintain.

Chandler describes his designs in this way: They are characterized by "clean lines, an absence of frills, and a heavy reliance on a geometric division of space. In an effort to imitate nature, a design based on curved lines often becomes a jumbled parody—fussy and unappealing. The strong lines featured in my work are meant to be softened in time by the plant material, but this unifying presence of the line is always felt, leaving the visitor with no doubt that it is indeed a landscape created by the human desire for order and beauty. I am also of the opinion that an outdoor space composed of straight lines will always be easier to take care of than a similar garden based on curved lines."

Chandler relies on expanses of lawn "as places for the eye to rest" and says that "it is a misconception that they are a high maintenance surface. The proper soil preparation, to a depth of at least 12 inches, coupled with the incorporation of plenty of organic matter, will cut lawn maintenance in half. The grass roots can penetrate deeper into the soil, tapping additional reserves of water and nutrients, particularly during periods of stress such as drought. I almost always use redwood 2 by 4s partially sunk in the ground at the edge of the lawn to reduce the need for hand edging. In all but the smallest gardens, a sprinkler system is a must, particularly in the arid parts of the country. I keep my system simple, with one type of sprinkler head for the lawn area and another for the shrub border. Put the whole system on a couple of time clocks, and work associated with watering is eliminated."

Over the years, Chandler has developed a list of plant material he describes as "old friends," among them: *Ilex* species, *Pittosporum tobira* 'Wheeler's Dwarf', *Platanus*

Naturally compact plants, geometric design, a limited color scheme, and the repeated use of the same varieties of plants are featured in the gardens of Jack Chandler, Landscape Architect, of St. Helena, California. The garden on these pages features dwarf pittosporum, agapanthus, India hawthorne, liquidambar, and potentilla ground cover.

Below: This outdoor eating area is the focal point of the garden. Plants used include star jasmine, Japanese maples,

agapanthus, Japanese privets in rear, tree fern, marigolds in raised planting bed, and pansies in pots.

Left: The plan of the garden shown on pages 12 and 13. An artful combination of paving and plants is the key to easy maintenance in this suburban Northern California condominium garden. 1. Potentilla verna (ground cover). 2. Southern yew pines. 3. Tree ferns. 4. Agapanthus. 5. Azaleas. 6. Baby's-tears. 7. Japanese maple. 8. Mayten trees. 9. Star jasmine. 10. Camellia. 11. Boxwood. 12. Dwarf azaleas. 13. Dwarf pittosporum. 14. Liquidambar. 15. India hawthorne. 16. Japanese privet (hedge). 17. Annuals in raised beds. A. Pool equipment vault. B. Swimming pool. C. Jacuzzi. D. Brick sitting area. E. Exposed aggregate paving. F. Brick paving. G. Dining area. H. Barbecue area. I. Front of house.

acerifolia, Trachelospermum jasminoides, Xylosma congestum, Vinca minor, Agapanthus 'Peter Pan', *Raphiolepis* species, and *Grevillea* 'Noellii'. "These plants have proven themselves to function admirably in a wide variety of climates and cultural conditions. They are attractive in both new and mature landscapes and my clients find them very easy to maintain.

"In short, I favor tailored, compact plants—from ground covers to trees. A compact, tight-leafed ground cover may take longer to cover an area, but in the long run it is far easier to maintain and harbors fewer slugs and snails than a larger-leafed, more open-growing choice. Fast-growing ground covers look rank in a hurry, requiring regular mowings and edging, and have a tendency to produce bare spots in their old age."

Dwarf or compact varieties of shrubs that are tolerant of both sun and shade conditions are featured in Chandler's landscapes for a good reason. "Don't get me wrong, I respect my clients' gardening abilities, but more often than not they are terrible at pruning—either neglecting the job entirely or doing it incorrectly. I've solved the problem by favoring compact shrubs that seldom need any pruning attention."

Chandler makes good use of trees, frequently in groups, and often limits himself to a single choice, repeated throughout the garden, stating that he "likes the continuity it produces." Trees that can be pollarded [cut back nearly to the trunk so as to produce dense masses of branches, "the simplest form of pruning," according to Chandler] are a favorite. The severe, yearly pruning produces trees of nearly equal shape and proportion, furthering the sense of continuity.

Although he likes color in the landscape, Chandler says that most of his clients simply aren't inclined to fuss with the routine of planting annuals. Instead of annuals, he uses flowering shrubs but limits the colors to one or two choices, such as mass plantings of raphiolepis and star jasmine: "the more color, the livelier the landscape, but all the more maintenance as well."

After the plant material is in place, Chandler always applies a preemergent weed killer and a ¾- to 1-inch layer of organic mulch over the beds or borders. "This gets the homeowner off to a good start for the first year or so, but I remind the client that the mulch should be renewed every year if it is to be a deterrent to weeds."

Robert C. Chesnut, Charleston, South Carolina

Robert Chesnut is a young, accomplished landscape architect whose work appears in a variety of settings throughout the Charleston area—from sophisticated city gardens to the more open surroundings of the suburbs. His clients are young couples with children, retired people, or single professionals, all of whom, more often than not, have one thing in common: They want a good looking garden without immoderate maintenance requirements. To that end, Chesnut has developed a series of questions and steps that apply to anyone interested in easy maintenance gardens.

First, he says, "Most people are afraid to hire a landscape architect because they think it'll be too expensive. What they don't realize is that they don't have to retain the person indefinitely. Anyone can afford an hour or two of consultation with a landscape architect. If you're just starting to plan, or are redesigning a garden, it's the best $100 you can spend. A landscape architect can give beginners important advice in three main areas: (1) where and how to start the project, (2) how much to expect to pay for various goods and services, and (3) names of reputable people to do such work as building fences and installing irrigation systems, brickwork, driveways, and plants.

"When I first meet with a client, I try to let them do all the talking. We go out into the yard and walk around the site. If they have difficulty expressing what they want, I ask them the following questions: (1) What problems do you have with the site as it now stands? (2) What do you plan to do with and in the garden? (3) What would you like to add in terms of structures and construction? (4) Do you have children? How many? (5) How much money have you allotted for the project? (6) Do you plan to live in the house indefinitely? (7) What type of life style do you enjoy? Travel frequently? Enjoy sports? Hate gardening? Enjoy gardening as a hobby? (8) How much time can you devote to gardening? (9) Do you plan to take care of the garden yourself or to have it taken care of professionally?

"It's a little like going to the doctor: The patient tells the doctor what the problems are, the doctor listens, and then formulates a solution. Additionally, I ask them how they visualize their outdoor surroundings in a

The gardens of Robert Chesnut, Landscape Architect, of Charleston, South Carolina, make good use of architectural and structural elements.

general sense, as predominantly decking or paving or covered in ground covers or lawn areas. Many times clients have not thought about designating a special area for children's play, an entertainment area for adults, or the possibility of opening up a room to a space in the garden that can be used as an extension of the house. Basically, I ask what they think they want and after interpreting their input, suggest what I think they need and what the demands of the site are."

If the client wants Chesnut to develop a design and supervise the installation, he divides the project into two distinct phases. This approach has many advantages, and do-it-yourselfers would do well to approach their own project in a similar fashion.

Chesnut refers to the first phase as the *construction plan.* At this point decisions are made concerning the size, placement,

and construction material required for fences, walls, pools, cabanas, dog runs, trash-can receptacles, mailbox details, walkways, driveways, patios, terraces, decks, lighting, guest parking, and service yards. This is also the stage at which he discusses ways to improve weak or undistinguished architectural features of the house, such as shutters, cupolas, window boxes, and porch railings; front-door alternatives; and color scheme changes. In short, any structural element that might complement or enhance the garden is attended to in the beginning.

Chesnut is the first to admit that he leans toward structural solutions to high maintenance problems; in a sense, he "builds" gardens. He says, "No garden is maintenance-free, but I am very conscious of designing a garden in such a way that the amount of time it takes to maintain it is limited. A brick patio or wooden deck will always be easier to maintain than a lawn, and a lawn with a well-constructed mowing strip is much easier to maintain than one without a definite edge. An attractive gazebo or arbor can add much the same charm to a garden that a quantity of high maintenance plant material would. In this regard, though, the easy-maintenance garden will always be more expensive to install than a traditional garden that relies almost exclusively on trees, shrubs, flowers, and vines to create beauty. In the long run, clients will save time *and* money on maintenance by constructing their gardens the way I do. And in the meantime, they have gardens that stay attractive through the years rather than gardens that get away from them."

In rating flooring surfaces, Chesnut gives asphalt and exposed aggregate the poorest

Seasonal color is confined to containers and brick-edged borders. From left to right, plants include impatiens, caladiums, and wax begonias under shade of crepe myrtles, backed by a brick wall covered with creeping fig. Begonias and petunias in pots. Geraniums in narrow bed along the length of the patio. Right border of annuals and perennials: roses, salvia, gloriosa daisy, phlox. Japanese holly against rear wall.

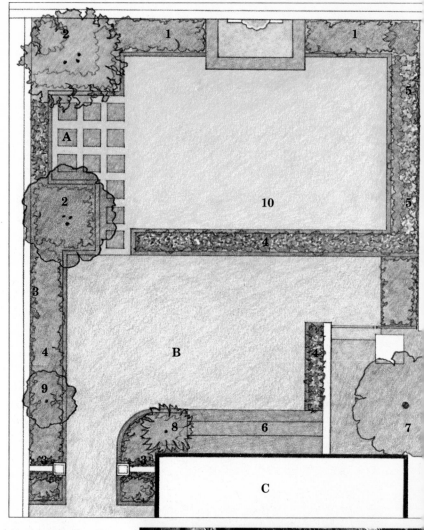

marks. "Asphalt is simply not a very satisfactory surface for use in the garden; and with exposed aggregate, the stones tend to dislodge over a period of time. Brick, flagstone, slate, and smooth-finish concrete make the best patios and terraces." Chesnut strongly recommends getting professional assistance in installing patios, decks, sidewalks, or driveways. "Bricks set on a base of sand tend to crack and often allow weeds to become established. The best method is to install bricks over a concrete base with mortar in between the bricks. This type of installation often requires the help of a professional."

After the structural elements are installed, Chesnut moves into the second phase: the *planting design*. Plants are used in Chesnut's gardens as a complement to the structural elements, "to soften the harshness of the construction using trees, using shrubs, ground covers, and some seasonal color."

The plants are chosen carefully, with Charleston's heat, humidity, wind, summer drought, and salt factor in mind. "Dwarf yaupon, any of the pittosporums, oleanders, crepe myrtle, wax myrtle, yews, and hollies have all performed admirably in our conditions, making few demands on their owner. In high wind areas, it's always best to shy away from brittle plants that may break easily, especially as they get more mature.

"Proper soil preparation is a must. In this area I always recommend that clients have their soil tested to see if there are any nutrient deficiencies. As a general practice, I add liberal amounts of peat moss, well-composted manure, and the recommended amounts of a balanced fertilizer to the soil before planting anything—from lawns to trees.

"For the person who wants to take up where the landscape architect leaves off after an hour or two of design and practical consultation, I recommend these initial steps: (1) Grade the site so there will be proper drainage away from the house; (2) get a lawn established, from sprigs, seed, or sod in a simple shape that will be easy to maintain; (3) concentrate plantings of trees and shrubs in the corners of the planting areas adjacent to lawn or paved areas. Mulch the areas between and fill in with plant material as need dictates and as you become more familiar with the type of plantings you want.

Above: The plan for the garden shown on pages 14 through 17. The solid architectural bones of the garden, and the easy maintenance permanent plants selected, mean that nearly all the time spent gardening is on the fun jobs. 1. Japanese holly. 2. Crepe myrtle underplanted with shade-loving annuals. 3. Creeping fig (against wall) 4. Annuals. 5. Perennials and annuals. 6. Annuals, herbs in pots. 7. Dogwood. 8. Fan palm. 9. Tea olive. 10. Lawn. A. Brick stepping stones. B. Brick patio. C. Service and storage area. Right: The inviting entrance to this small garden is achieved with two brick pillars covered with creeping fig.

lawns and flower beds or borders; limit the selection of plants used right next to the house to those that are naturally low growing or compact; plant large areas in a single plant choice; use flat areas for lawns or ground covers and sloping areas for flowers or shrubs (slopes are difficult to mow); choose plants that work with nature, that is, hardy plants that grow easily in your climate and that may readily reseed or, in the case of bulbs, that can be naturalized, thereby eliminating seasonal replanting to a great extent.

"Our gardens can stand a certain amount of benign neglect. Divisions between plantings within the borders or beds are allowed to shift as one plant or another dominates an area. These gardens rarely look identical from one year to the next. They are the opposite of neatly clipped, severely ordered landscapes, which are basically high maintenance in their rigidity and boring in their sameness from one season to the next.

"Not particularly related to maintenance but also important is that we almost always plant the garden with a view from inside the house in mind. Because these gardens are beautiful for much of the year, keeping indoor viewing in mind allows the garden to be appreciated even though it may be too cold to go outside. Another aside: We always use big or bold plants in small gardens to keep them from becoming overly 'precious' or pretty-pretty. Nothing makes a small garden look smaller than the use of a lot of small plants."

Like most landscape architects interested in easy maintenance, Oehme and van Sweden take great pains to ensure that the soil is well prepared before planting anything (see pages 45 and 46). Because they encourage the flowers to reseed themselves naturally, they don't use any preemergent weed killers. In their place, Oehme and van Sweden use a 3- or 4-inch layer of shredded hardwood mulch, which they say is "wonderful for increasing water retention, producing humus in the soil, deterring weeds, and is beautiful to look at and delightful to smell at the same time."

They say their gardens are more work the first year than any other, but once the plants are established, the care is very simple. "Except at the change of seasons, I don't spend more than an hour a month maintaining my own garden," says van Sweden. "The most

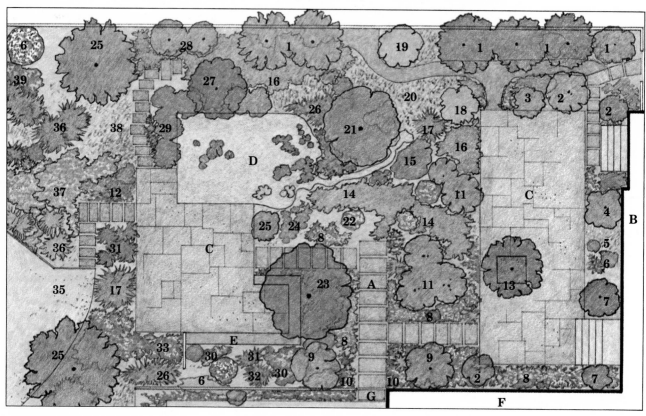

important thing is to do a thorough cleaning in spring; then add a fresh layer of mulch. If you do this, your maintenance chores for the rest of the year will be greatly reduced. The big maintenance push is in late winter—cutting all the grasses down, mulching, and generally cleaning up. This takes about five or six hours, but that's all it takes. We favor plants that seldom need dividing, so the one maintenance headache with perennials is not a problem."

SUMMING UP

If we can generally summarize what we have learned from these inside views of the professional approach, we come up with two main ideas. All of the participants agreed on (1) the need for a strong, unifying design, and (2) the importance of proper and thorough soil preparation before planting anything.

Bold design with a distinct division of space invites organization and simplicity. It was once suggested that one way to make an easy maintenance garden was to start with a plan on paper showing the entire area covered in decking, a pavement, or some other nonliving surface. Then thoughtfully remove areas of paving for the plantings you feel are the minimum needed for comfort, privacy, and beauty. While most designers would say that this is a somewhat brutal approach, it does point out that ar-

riving at real solutions to maintenance problems requires looking at the landscape in a new way. We discuss all these design questions in Chapter 3.

Unless you are one of the lucky minority who has a garden with a naturally occurring good loam soil, adequate soil preparation before planting is a must. Some of the instructions, given on pages 45 and 46, may seem a bit fussy at first, but long-term easy maintenance is practically impossible without following them.

Below and bottom: Two details of the garden, showing wide use of grasses, sedums, heathers, and yucca.

Opposite page: The plan for the garden featured on pages 20 through 23. Gardens by Oehme, van Sweden & Associates, Landscape Architects, of Washington, D.C., use masses of a great number of plants. The resulting gardens have a distinct character of intricate but easy to maintain beauty. 1. Canadian hemlock. 2. Japanese holly. 3. Pyracantha. 4. Bull Bay magnolia. 5. Lily turf. 6. Plume poppy. 7. Euonymus. 8. Showy sedum. 9. Devil's walking stick. 10. Blue plumbago. 11. Mugo pine. 12. Blue fescue. 13. Dove tree. 14. Prostrate juniper. 15. Japanese knotweed. 16. English ivy. 17. Giant eulalia grass. 18. Nellie Stevens holly. 19. Fraser photina. 20. Epimedium. 21. American hornbeam. 22. Siberian iris. 23. Chinese maackia. 24. Cardinal flower. 25. Austrian pine. 26. Sedge. 27. Purple osier willow. 28. Hicks yews. 29. Evergreen honeysuckle. 30. Black-eyed Susan. 31. Yucca. 32. Reed grass. 33. St. John's wort. 34. Lawn. 35. Mixed grasses. 36. Heaths and heathers. 37. Siberian bugloss. 38. Purple loosestrife. A. Bark path. B. Residence. C. Bluestone terrace. D. Lily pond. E. Bench. F. Garage. G. To driveway.

ARRIVING AT A FINAL PLAN— THE FOUR ELEMENTS

Once you have decided on a basic design that you like and that suits your needs, it's time to get specific concerning exact dimension, building materials, and plant selection. To keep your thinking simple, we have broken the elements you'll need to include in your plan into four categories: floors, walls, ceilings, and plant material. Examples of many easy maintenance possibilities in each of these categories follow. Refer to these pages often as you finalize your plan to spark new ideas and to keep you on the easy maintenance trail.

Floors

The homeowner in search of an easy maintenance garden should make outdoor floor-ing choices with extreme care. Next to your choice of plant material, floors are the single most important element in determining how much maintenance a garden will require in the long run. There is a great difference, for example, between the amount of maintenance required by a brick patio and the requirements of a newly planted lawn or similar ground cover. But each choice has its unique benefits and drawbacks, depending on its intended use.

Different types of garden floors can be appropriate for different parts of the garden. The decision-making process should begin with a series of questions: Will the areas receive a lot of traffic? Do you need a surface for young children to play on? Is the area going to be used as an outdoor kitchen or dining area? As a place to sunbathe? Does

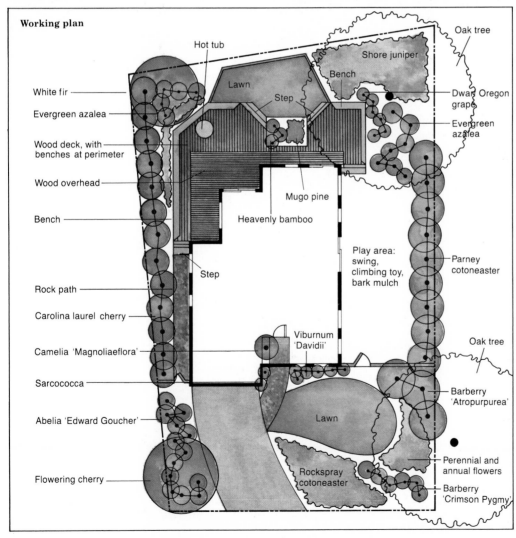

Working plan

White fir
Evergreen azalea
Wood deck, with benches at perimeter
Wood overhead
Bench
Rock path
Carolina laurel cherry
Camelia 'Magnoliaeflora'
Sarcococca
Abelia 'Edward Goucher'
Flowering cherry

Hot tub
Lawn
Step
Step
Mugo pine
Heavenly bamboo
Play area: swing, climbing toy, bark mulch
Viburnum 'Davidii'
Lawn
Rockspray cotoneaster

Oak tree
Shore juniper
Bench
Dwarf Oregon grape
Evergreen azalea
Parney cotoneaster
Oak tree
Barberry 'Atropurpurea'
Perennial and annual flowers
Barberry 'Crimson Pygmy'

A working drawing is the final step in the planning and design process. From these drawings, you should have all the information necessary to install the landscape. The information should be as exact and detailed as possible. Measurements, names and spacing of plants, the type of lumber for fences and decks, and any other important information should be included. If the working drawing is done on tracing paper, it's easy to have several blueprints made.

the terrain of your yard make establishing any flat surface difficult?

The choices of flooring material break down easily into two main groups: living and nonliving. There are many nonliving choices, the main differences among which are aesthetics, cost, and ease of installation. Living choices are plentiful as well, but if the area is to receive much foot traffic, the choice is limited to grass lawns and a very few sturdy, low-growing ground covers. If the area will not be walked or played on, the choice expands to include the full range of both low- and tall-growing ground covers.

In all but the smallest gardens, several flooring choices, both living and nonliving, can be used together, often with very attractive results. As we have previously mentioned, be wary of covering too much of your garden floor with a nonliving surface. Wide expanses of concrete, wood, or brick should be relieved by areas left open for plants or trees. On the other hand, too large an area devoted to lawns or some ground covers can quickly result in considerable maintenance chores. Be guided by the idea of *balance,* an important concept from the standpoint of both beauty and maintenance.

Give due attention to the shape of the floor. Most landscape architects and designers agree that the simpler the overall shape, the better the garden will look and the easier the floor, if planted in living material, will be to take care of. Straight-line geometric shapes are favored by many designers, but curved shapes can be equally satisfactory if the curves are open and flowing rather than a series of complicated twists and tight turns.

Special Considerations for Lawns and Ground Covers. For many people, weeding, watering, mowing, edging, and fertilizing just don't add up to easy maintenance. And there's no denying that these and other chores are a necessary part of having a well-kept lawn. But stop and think for a moment of what the lawn gives in return.

No other part of the landscape has quite as powerful an effect as a lawn. In most cases, it is the element that ties the entire garden scene together, and it does it beautifully.

Aside from its effect on design, a lawn is also a tremendously versatile garden surface. For playing, picnics, dozing, or gym-

nastics, there is nothing quite like a lawn. And could there possibly be a better surface to catch the play of shadow and light, changing with every hour?

If you have correctly prepared the soil (see pages 45 and 46) and seeded, sprigged, or sodded the new lawn with the grass variety best adapted to your climate and growing conditions, you are well on your way to a lawn that will require less maintenance than usual. There are other steps you should consider to make subsequent lawn maintenance even easier.

Mowing and edging are two jobs that are done time and time again, and any inefficiency here will add up. The lawns that are the easiest to mow are level and geometric in design. You will also find that an unbroken expanse of lawn—no sundials, flower beds, tall sprinkler heads, trees, or paths to get in the way—is less tedious to mow. And an edging strip of wood, concrete, or brick will save countless hours of back-annoying work (see pages 47 and 48).

If you are in the planning stages of a new lawn or are about to change an existing one, plan your lawn to be an even number of square feet or close to it. You will have less trouble figuring out fertilizer, insecticide, fungicide, and soil conditioner application rates.

You will probably want to consult the Ortho book *All About Lawns* for guidance in choosing a grass that is right for your design and right for your climate. This book gives complete information on all aspects of grass selection and lawn installation and care.

The Choices. Discussed on the next two pages are ten choices of flooring materials for gardens. We have briefly noted the pros and cons of each and given general indications about costs. Prices, of course, will vary by geographic area, and over a period of time they are likely to increase. If any of the surfaces are particularly adapted for do-it-yourself projects, this too is noted.

Top: Lawns are a great surface for playing and tumbling—just ask any kid. Above: One of the best ways to keep lawns from becoming a maintenance headache is to establish a distinct edge, like this brick border.

Several flooring choices, from bottom left, clockwise: Brick-edged asphalt; old paving stones; unglazed tile set in sand; gravel and stepping stones; concrete with built-in border; and a ground cover combination of violets and false Solomon's seal.

FLOORING CHOICES

Floors are the most important element in any landscape, easy maintenance or not. They not only represent the most significant elements in terms of maintenance, but they are also the most obvious part of the landscape—the part you see first. The most obvious easy maintenance choices are the nonliving surfaces such as concrete, brick, or bark; but any floor choice should be determined on the basis of aesthetics as well. When you make your choices, keeping easy maintenance in mind, don't forget to consider the color, texture, and pattern of the floor and how it will blend with the other elements in the garden. Some of the most successful gardens combine a variety of flooring without forsaking the goal of easy maintenance.

Concrete. Concrete slabs for use as patios are probably the most popular, practical, adaptable, and economical of all paved surfaces. Installing concrete slabs is within the reach of most do-it-yourselfers. As an option, a concrete mason can be hired to do the job from start to finish without incurring immoderate expense.

Popular ways to add color and texture to concrete are either to expose the aggregate or inlay stone in the surface or to make geometric patterns out of brick or wood borders. Without these variations, concrete can be a cold and uninteresting surface.

Wood. Wood is most often thought of in relation to making decks. At current prices, a wooden deck is about twice as expensive as concrete. But decks, unlike concrete or brick patios, are not limited to level land, and they can be placed just about anywhere that's appropriate, regardless of terrain.

Wood is perfectly at home in the garden—one of the most natural surfaces possible for outdoor living. With its inherent decay-resistant qualities, redwood is the favored lumber choice; but other woods will suffice as long as they have been treated to resist decay. Deck building does not require high-level carpentry skills.

Asphalt. Asphalt can be appropriate in the garden, especially when its use is limited. Large expanses of asphalt tend to dominate and make an area look like nothing so much as a parking lot; so it is a good idea to disguise it in some fashion. It can be used in spots that are not on center stage or, to lessen its impact, broken into a small grid pattern using wood borders. Softer than concrete, it's a good play surface for children and ideal for service areas. It is not suitable, however, as a surface on which to set chairs; as the sun heats the asphalt, it softens, and furniture will mar it. Generally speaking, asphalt is not a do-it-yourself surface.

Brick. Bricks are perhaps the first choice for garden floors if only because of their long-time association with beautiful gardens. They are one of the most expensive choices. Three kinds are available: new bricks, used bricks (with a weathered look), and the relatively new "pavers," which look like regular bricks but are only half as thick. Bricks and pavers can be laid in a variety of patterns over a bed of sand without mortar or on top of concrete with mortar. Bricks on sand are easily dislodged or their pattern disturbed by a variety of forces, including roots, wear, and freezing and thawing. For the most permanent surface, professionals recommend setting bricks in concrete. With this method, installing bricks is an ideal do-it-yourself project because bricks are easy to handle and the installation can be done in stages.

Tiles. Tiles can be used for a terrace or patio, especially in a Mediterranean-style garden. Unglazed tiles are best, because glazed tiles are extremely slippery when wet. Clay tiles blend in with both rustic and formal landscapes. However, they have to be carefully laid on a cement bed, over absolutely level terrain, and then mortared together. Gardeners should be prepared to allot sufficient time to do the job well or consider having them professionally installed. Clay tiles are among the most expensive of flooring choices. Concrete tiles, even when installed in an interesting pattern, are more easily laid than clay tiles. They can simply be placed in a level bed of gravel and sand.

Gravel. For the sake of clarity, we will refer here to only three of the many types of gravel, all of which are good flooring surfaces in the right places. Pea gravel, one choice, suffers from a lowly reputation, but anyone who's visited some of the formal gardens of Europe will quickly attest to its functional stylishness when used with sensitivity. It's a clean surface that when applied in depths of 3 inches or more all but eliminates weed growth. Gravel that is a combination of small stones, sand, and clay, sometimes referred to as *road base*, is another flooring choice, perhaps less aesthetically appealing than some but nevertheless effective when used in limited areas. To work in a permanent traffic area, it should be applied in a layer at least 3–4 inches thick and well compacted. A flooring of smooth river stones in varying sizes has been a popular easy maintenance choice for a number of years, so popular, in fact, that its appeal may be diminishing from overuse. Although this floor is difficult to walk on and unsuitable as a surface on which to place patio furniture, it is useful for low-traffic and outlying garden areas. When combined with a few big rocks and a limited but appropriate plant selection, as in arid-climate landscaping, it can be quite attractive. Most people prefer to lay a black polyethylene film under a 2- or 3-inch layer of stones for complete weed control and the last word in easy maintenance flooring. All gravel flooring is easy and inexpensive to install.

Bark. Bark is available in bags at most garden centers and nurseries and in some locations in bulk. Three or four grades, from fine to coarse, are commonly offered. The coarsest is suitable for use as a mulch in flower beds or borders; finer grades are more appropriate for areas that will receive foot traffic. Bark makes a good flooring choice for children's play areas, but it has a tendency to scatter and disintegrate over a period of time. Yearly applications are usually necessary to maintain the original thickness of the surface. Redwood bark weathers from its rather garish original red color to a more appealing silvery gray in a matter of a few months. Bark is easy and inexpensive to install.

Lawns. Lawns are unquestionably the most popular and versatile of all flooring choices for the garden, and for good reason. Despite regular maintenance demands, some people feel that nothing can compare to a lawn in terms of beauty, suitability, and the way it complements and unifies any landscape. Your decision to use a lawn as a floor will be based on whether you think that the returns justify the effort required. Speaking strictly from an economic point of view (in areas where the cost of water is not prohibitive), lawns are one of the least expensive high-traffic flooring choices.

Lawn Substitutes. If the area will not receive traffic, any of the compact ground covers such as *Vinca minor,* Irish and Scotch moss, and the small-leafed ivies can work as a visual substitute for a grass lawn and have fewer demands. Lawn substitutes are slightly more expensive to install than grass lawns, but they make up for the added expense in being easier to maintain.

Tall Ground Covers. As a flooring choice, tall ground covers such as junipers, liriope, and daylilies, are somewhat misnamed. They do not invite nor can they withstand traffic; and they do not fulfill any other use commonly associated with floors. Tall ground covers are a means to an end, and more often than not, they are used to cover out-of-the-way problem areas. This does not mean that they are not attractive. Chosen and placed carefully, tall ground covers can bring color and texture to an otherwise unappealing spot.

Three very different types of garden walls. Above left: A standard wooden fence with attractive finish details, top and bottom. The ground cover of blue plumbago is allowed to spill naturally over the apshalt drive. Top right: A wire fence, all but forgotten under a heavy cover of ivy. Above: A traditional solid brick wall.

Walls

When landscape architects and designers talk about walls in the garden, they are generally referring to any vertical surface that blocks the view, either completely or partly. The wall most common in the garden is a fence, but other landscape elements may work in the same way: a hedge, a group of tall shrubs, the neighbor's garage, an honest-to-goodness stone or brick wall.

From an easy maintenance point of view, the best walls are structural, constructed of wood, metal, wire, or brick. Walls or fences provide privacy, support vines, protect against strong winds, create comfortably warm spots in sunny areas, and add horizontal or vertical interest. A wall can also be a unifying element if it is constructed of a material that harmonizes with the house. Shown on these pages are a number of walls made from a variety of materials in a variety of styles. You can add to this list of possibilities. As you drive through different neighborhoods or tour new areas, keep an eye open for fences and walls that might be appropriate for your own situation.

CHOICES FOR WALLS

Wood. Wood is the most versatile material for constructing walls or fences. Imagine for a moment these possibilities: the standard "good neighbor" fence made from 1- by 10-inch lumber; an old-fashioned lath, lattice-work fence painted the same color as the house; a solid, shingled fence with a wide cap on top for a finished look; the charm of a wide picket fence surrounding a front-yard garden; or a fence with boards spaced regularly to allow a partial view while still giving a sense of privacy. There's literally no end to the types and styles of fences that can be constructed from wood. If you're in need of inspiration, large lumber yards usually display short sections of a variety of wooden fence styles. Wooden fences, while not inexpensive, represent a good value in terms of easy maintenance and longevity. Even gardeners whose skills are rudimentary find it possible to construct walls using wood.

Brick. Brick is pleasing to look at, but owing to its expense, few people create a wall or fence entirely of this material. Most decide on a combination of materials, using brick for the base and posts and filling in with panels of lattice, ornamental ironwork, or wood. Built to last a lifetime, brick walls are a garden tradition.

Wire. Wire fences are popular because they are easy to install and relatively inexpensive. They do need some "dressing up," however, to tone down or eliminate the industrial look. Consider using wood posts and an ornamental wood cap to make a wire fence more gardenesque. A wire fence is an ideal support for vines, which can quickly transform it into a thing of beauty. Another method for making a wire fence less obtrusive is to paint it black or dark green; the wire almost disappears as you look through it. Putting up a wire fence is definitely within the range of the do-it-yourselfer, but take care to stretch the wire tightly between its supports so that it does not sag or bow with the passage of time.

Traditional Hedge. A traditional hedge formed of needled evergreens or small-leafed deciduous shrubs ranks low on the list of easy maintenance walls. Quite simply, such a hedge requires regular shearing to look its best. If the hedge is at all extensive, this means a considerable chore two or three times a year. Still, if you inherit a mature hedge in an already planted garden, it should be respected as one of the most attractive of all garden walls.

Informal Hedge. A planting of tall-growing shrubs such as English laurel, oleander, and many of the pittosporum, in a more or less straight line, can work in much the same way that a traditional hedge does, but it will not require the same level of maintenance. Tall-growing shrubs left to grow their own way don't have the formal appearance of a clipped hedge but are attractive in their own right, especially in large gardens. As with any living wall or fence, gardeners have to be patient while the shrubs attain their final size.

Hedges. The landscape wall requiring the most maintenance is a traditional needled or leafy hedge. For hedges to look their best, they need regular shearing and more or less constant, general care. Less demanding is a group of tall-growing shrubs planted in a straight or semistraight line. The fact that they can be left unsheared, free to establish their natural form, saves the gardener considerable time and effort. They can be evergreen or deciduous and may flower or not, depending on your choice. You might decide on a deciduous variety if you want a tall shrub to screen an undesirable view during the summer months when you are most often in the garden. When it loses its leaves in winter, it will still provide some screening and allow the low, winter sun to play over that part of your garden that otherwise might not get much natural light. The bare skeletons of shrubs in winter can have a sculpted appearance and be particularly pleasing to look at. We have listed some popular possibilities for living walls on this page.

An informal group of shrubs—star jasmine, Japanese privet, and cherry laurel, left unsheared—screens out the nearby road next to this entrance walk.

Using Vines. If you decide to construct a wall rather than plant one, don't overlook the softening effect of vines. Vines can transform a wooden fence or masonry wall into a green, leafy surface—much like a hedge—with considerably less maintenance required. For the most part, vines are quick growers, bringing color, fragrance, and interest to any vertical surface in a hurry.

This spacious garden was designed by Andropogon Associates of Philadelphia for a natural look, using mostly native plants. Ostrich fern springs up around the strategically-placed rock. In the distance right, double-file viburnum; in the distance left, bridal-wreath spirea.

Ceilings

The most beautiful ceiling for outdoor rooms—and the one requiring the least maintenance—is, as you might guess, the sky, whether it's blue, mottled with clouds, or overcast. Outdoor space is usually open to the elements, but it is almost always desirable to create a place in the landscape that's protected from the effects of sun, rain, and wind.

When asked to come up with ideas for ceilings in the garden, most people immediately think of a canopy of leaves from a large, overhanging tree. There's no doubt that a gracefully arching tree is one of the loveliest ceilings in the garden, but many trees also require the most attention. So choose trees that are pest-free and don't require spraying. Many trees need no pruning other than initial training; and if they are clean, or underplanted with a deep ground cover, there are no leaves to rake.

The most satisfactory trees for the easy maintenance landscape are those that will thrive in the natural conditions of your yard. The best bet is to limit yourself to those species that adapt best to your particular climate and that answer your specific design requirements. Easy maintenance trees are listed on page 39.

Structural ceilings. Structural ceilings can be constructed from a variety of widely available materials, including wood, lath lattice, canvas, plastic and fiberglass, and bamboo and reed screening. From a maintenance standpoint, you should take the du-rability of the material into consideration. Canvas and screening of either bamboo or reed both need to be replaced periodically. Wooden ceilings, whether solid or open, fit nicely into a garden setting, especially after they weather. Synthetic materials, such as plastic and fiberglass, are considered by many people to be less aesthetically pleasing, but transparent panels overhead can ensure complete privacy from upstairs windows (either your own or your neighbors'), soften the light, and when viewed from underneath, display interesting patterns created by overhanging tree limbs and leaves.

If you make your overhead structure solid, you'll have complete shade, but you'll also have a structure that traps warm air. In areas with hot summers, the lack of ventilation may make the enclosure uninviting. Usually it is a better idea to make a ceiling with regular openings, which allow ventilation and create interesting light and shade patterns on the floor below.

Plant Material

Plants always have been and always will be the basis for a garden. No matter how rigorous your goals, you will need plants to transform any area into a garden.

There is a relatively new trend in thinking about plant material that makes the plants themselves easier to take care of. Instead of using many varieties of plants, most of the landscape architects and designers we talked to favored mass plantings or groups of the same type of plant. In addition to making maintenance easier, mass plantings also make a much stronger design statement than similar-sized plantings of unrelated plants.

From a maintenance perspective, there is a good reason for planning a garden around this idea: Watering, fertilizing, and pest and disease control can all be taken care of at the same time and in the same way. This economy adds up to easy maintenance, pure and simple. But if a garden made up of a limited number of different plants is not your idea of a garden at all, don't be influenced by current trends to create a garden that you don't like. Whatever your decisions, you should choose plants well suited to your climate and cultural conditions, those whose mature size is in scale with the allotted space.

When it comes time to choose plant ma-terial for your garden, consult the lists on the following pages. We have broken plants into six general categories to make selection easier: Trees, shrubs, ground covers, flowering plants, drought-tolerant plants, and plants that need little or no pruning. Plants that appear in these lists under each heading can be found in the Plant Selection Guide starting on page 73.

A final bit of advice when choosing plant material for an easy maintenance garden: Always favor the new varieties of old favorites. Plant breeders are constantly working to develop new varieties of plants that are more resistant to damage from pests and diseases and that are naturally more compact and neater than their ancestors. Improved varieties almost invariably mean less work for the gardener.

CEILING CHOICES

Trees. It's possible to create an entire garden using a grove planting of all the same type of tree. You do not need a large space; all you need is enough space to plant six or more trees relatively close together. This type of planting, as it matures, can provide one of the finest and most appealing outdoor ceilings imaginable. Plan to leave room in the center of the grove for a picnic table, a garden seat, or a hammock. On a warm summer day, a grove will act as a magnet, pulling you to its interior. Almost any tree will adapt to grove planting, but some require more work than others. See our list of easy maintenance trees for suggestions, and remember to keep the trees pruned up high, above eye level, to control their growth.

The old-fashioned shade tree with its spreading limbs is another option for creating a leafy ceiling in your garden. One word of warning, however: Trees sold as shade makers, such as the silver maple, fruitless mulberry, and tree-of-heaven, are fast growers, so fast that pruning is necessary on a yearly basis to keep them well shaped and healthy. Whenever you plant a living ceiling, you can expect the regular maintenance chores of sweeping and raking, but as one of our consultants put it, "You have to expect a tree to behave like a tree." Fast growing or not, living ceilings are not instant ceilings; if you need shade in a hurry, consider a ceiling made of wood, canvas, or synthetic panels.

Wood and Reeds. A ceiling constructed of wood or a combination of wood and reeding can be as simple or as complex as you would like to make it. A simple wooden frame supported by posts can serve as the framework for any number of nat-ural ceiling materials, including bamboo screening or rolled reed screening. Once the framework is constructed, it's easy and inexpensive to attach the desired ceiling material. Bear in mind that most natural materials available in rolls will require replacement every other year. A more permanent and more expensive alternative is a ceiling constructed of lumber, from lath to heavier timbers such as 2 by 6s laid on end with plenty of space in between for air circulation and to create a changing shadow pattern.

Plastic and Fiberglass. Plastic and fiberglass, available in 4- by 8-foot sheets, were specifically developed for use as outdoor building material. Although the presence of one of these synthetic materials in the garden can be an overwhelming one, either is an inexpensive, carefree, and easy-to-use material for ceilings. The main drawback, aside from lack of aesthetic appeal, is that air circulation is inhibited. Keep this factor in mind, particularly if you live in a hot-weather climate.

Canvas. Canvas ceilings are not in the do-it-yourself class, but they are an attractive alternative if money is no object. Canvas has a long history of use in garden situations; nothing can quite match its crisp, elegant appearance. Its primary drawbacks, besides its expense, are two: Unless specially treated, it needs to be replaced every four or five years; and it casts complete shade and reduces air circulation if it is installed in a solid panel. You can, however, have the canvas installed in bands or other patterns to allow regular open spaces. Canvas is available in a wide variety of colors and patterns to suit a variety of garden styles.

EASY MAINTENANCE PLANTS FOR SPECIAL PURPOSES

All of the plants in the following lists have sufficient manners to qualify them as easy maintenance plants. Seen from a different perspective, however, they contribute to the melange of sensual delights found only in the garden. This may be a poet's response to practicality, but it is as legitimate a concern as any other. Look in the Plant Selection Guide, beginning on page 73, for more information on each plant.

Trees

Evergreen
Acacia baileyana
Eucalyptus species
Ilex vomitoria
Laurus nobilis
Thuja occidentalis

Deciduous
Alnus rhombifolia
Betula nigra
Carpinus betulus
Celtis species
Cercidiphyllum japonicum
Elaeagnus angustifolia
Ginkgo biloba
Koelreuteria paniculata
Liquidambar styraciflua
Nyssa sylvatica
Ostrya virginiana
Phellodendron amurense
Platanus acerifolia
Pyrus calleryana
Tilia americana
Zelkova serrata

Ground covers

Tall (over 6 inches)
Achillea species
Alyssum saxatile
Arctotheca calendula
Armeria species
Athyrium species
Ceanothus species
Cistus species
Convallaria majalis
Cotoneaster species
Euonymus fortunei
Heaths and Heathers
Hedera species
Hemerocallis species
Hosta species
Juniperus species
Lantana species
Leptospermum scoparium
Liriope species
Ophiopogon japonicus
Osteospermum fruticosum
Pachysandra terminalis
Paxistima canbyi
Rosmarinus officinalis
Vinca species

Lagerstroemia indica

Lawn Substitutes
(6 inches and under)
Ajuga species
Arabis species
Arctostaphylos uva-ursi
Gazania species
Heaths and Heathers
Hedera species
Juniperus species
Lobularia maritima
Lysimachia nummularia
Sagina subulata
Soleirolia soleirolii
Vinca species

Drought-Tolerant Plants

Achillea species
Alyssum saxatile
Arabis species
Aronia arbutifolia
Berberis thunbergii
Callistemon citrinus
Carpinus betulus
Ceanothus species
Celtis species
Chaenomeles speciosa
Cistus species
Coreopsis tinctoria
Elaeagnus angustifolia
Elaeagnus pungens
Eschscholzia californica
Euonymus fortunei
Fothergilla major
Genista tinctoria
Hemerocallis species
Juniperus species

Kniphofia uvaria
Lagerstroemia indica
Nandina domestica
Nerium oleander
Osteospermum fruticosum
Phellodendron amurense
Portulaca grandiflora
Rudbeckia hirta var.
pulcherima
Sedum species
Sempervivum tectorum
Xylosma congestum

Plants That Need Little or No Pruning

Clethra alnifolia
Cotoneaster species
Eucalyptus species
Euonymus alatus
Fothergilla major
Genista tinctoria
Grevillea 'Noellii'
Heaths and Heathers
Hypericum prolificum
Ilex cornuta
Ilex vomitoria
Juniperus species
Koelreuteria paniculata
Laurus nobilis
Leptospermum scoparium
Nandina domestica
Osmanthus fragrans
Ostrya virginiana
Pittosporum tobira
Raphiolepis indica
Tilia americana

Shrubs for Easy Maintenance

Evergreens
Abelia × *grandiflora*
Aucuba japonica
Callistemon citrinus
Ceanothus species
Cistus species
Cotoneaster species
Elaeagnus pungens
Escallonia × *exoniensis*
Grevillea 'Noellii'
Heaths and Heathers
Ilex cornuta
Ilex vomitoria
Juniperus species
Leptospermum scoparium
Ligustrum species
Nandina domestica
Nerium oleander
Osmanthus fragrans
Pinus mugo var. *mugo*
Pittosporum tobira
Raphiolepis indica
Rosmarinus officinalis
Trachelospermum species
Viburnum species
Xylosma congestum

Deciduous
Aronia arbutifolia
Berberis thunbergii
Calycanthus floridus
Caragana arborescens
Chaenomeles speciosa
Clethra alnifolia
Deutzia gracilis
Euonymus alatus
Fothergilla major
Genista tinctoria
Hamamelis × *intermedia*
Hypericum prolificum
Kerria japonica
Lagerstroema indica
Myrica pensylvanica
Philadelphus coronarius
Rhus copallina
Spiraea species
Viburnum species

Flowering Plants

Annuals and Perennials
Acanthus mollis
Achillea species
Agapanthus species
Alyssum saxatile
Arctotheca calendula
Armeria species
Asclepias tuberosa
Calendula officinalis
Coreopsis tinctoria
Eschscholzia californica
Gaillardia pulchella
Gazania species
Hemerocallis species
Kniphofia uvaria
Lantana species
Lavandula angustifolia
Liatris spicata
Liriope species
Lobularia maritima
Lysimachia nummularia
Pelargonium × *hortorum*
Petunia × *hybrida*
Portulaca grandiflora
Rudbeckia hirta var. *pulcherima*
Salvia species
Sedum species
Sempervivum tectorum
Tagetes species
Tropaeolum majus
Zinnia species

Shrubs
Abelia × *grandiflora*
Caragana arborescens
Ceanothus species
Chaenomeles speciosa
Clethra alnifolia
Deutzia gracilis
Escallonia × *exoniensis*
Fothergilla major
Genista tinctoria
Grevillea 'Noellii'
Hamamelis × *intermedia*
Heaths and Heathers
Hypericum prolificum
Kerria japonica
Lagerstroemia indica
Leptospermum scoparium
Ligustrum species
Nandina domestica
Nerium oleander
Osmanthus fragrans
Philadelphus coronarius
Raphiolepis indica
Rosmarinus officinalis
Spiraea species
Trachelospermum species
Viburnum species

Trees
Acacia baileyana
Elaeagnus angustifolia
Eucalyptus species
Koelreuteria paniculata
Pyrus calleryana
Tilia americana

Ground Covers
Ajuga species
Arabis species
Arctostaphylos uva-ursi
Ceanothus species
Cistus species
Convallaria majalis
Heaths and Heathers
Lantana species
Leptospermum scoparium
Lobularia maritima
Lysimachia nummularia
Ophiopogon japonicus
Osteospermum fruticosum
Rosmarinus officinalis
Trachelospermum species
Vinca species

Fruiting Plants

Arctostaphylos uva-ursi
Aronia arbutifolia
Betula nigra
Carpinus betulus
Celtus species
Cercidiphyllum japonicum
Cotoneaster species
Elaeagnus angustifolia
Elaeagnus pungens
Ilex cornuta
Ilex vomitoria
Koelreuteria paniculata
Laurus nobilis
Ligustrum species
Liriope species
Myrica pensylvanica
Ophiopogon japonicus
Platanus acerifolia
Tilia americana
Viburnum species

Plants with Showy Flowers

Abelia × *grandiflora*
Acanthus mollis
Achillea species
Agapanthus species
Alyssum saxatile
Arctotheca calendula
Asclepias tuberosa
Calendula officinalis
Ceanothus species
Chaenomeles speciosa
Cistus species
Coreopsis tinctoria
Deutzia gracilis
Escallonia × *exoniensis*
Eschscholzia californica
Gaillardia pulchella
Gazania species
Genista tinctoria
Hemerocallis species
Hypericum prolificum
Kniphofia uvaria
Koelreuteria paniculata
Lagerstroemia indica
Lantana species
Liatris spicata
Liriope species
Nerium oleander
Osteospermum fruticosum
Pelargonium × *hortorum*
Petunia × *hybrida*
Portulaca grandiflora
Raphiolepis indica
Rudbeckia hirta var. *pulcherima*
Salvia species
Spiraea species
Tagetes species
Tropaeolum majus
Vinca species
Zinnia species

Plants for Fall Color

Berberis thunbergii
Carpinus betulus
Cercidiphyllum japonicum
Clethra alnifolia
Euonymus alatus
Fothergilla major
Ginkgo biloba
Hamamelis × *intermedia*
Lagerstroemia indica
Liquidambar styraciflua
Nyssa sylvatica
Pyrus calleryana
Rhus copallina
Viburnum species
Zelkova serrata

Plants with Fragrant Flowers

Calycanthus floridus
Clethra alnifolia
Convallaria majalis
Elaeagnus angustifolia
Elaeagnus pungens
Escallonia × *exoniensis*
Fothergilla major
Hamamelis × *intermedia*
Lobularia maritima
Osmanthus fragrans
Petunia × *hybrida*
Philadelphus coronarius
Tilia americana
Trachelospermum species
Tropaeolum majus
Viburnum species

Plants with Aromatic Foliage

Achillea species
Calendula officinalis
Callistemon citrinus
Cistus species
Eucalyptus species
Laurus nobilis
Lavandula angustifolia
Leptospermum scoparium
Myrica pensylvanica
Pelargonium × *hortorum*
Rosmarinus officinalis
Tagetes species

Plants with Attractive Winter Silhouettes

Alnus rhombifolia
Betula nigra
Cercidiphyllum japonicum
Elaeagnus angustifolia
Kerria japonica
Lagerstroemia indica
Phellodendron amurense
Platanus acerifolia
Rhus copallina

NATURAL LANDSCAPES: AN ALTERNATIVE

In recent years there has been a movement in landscaping toward making home landscapes more compatible with the climate and terrain in which they occur and more in keeping with an appropriate historical framework. In essence, gardens growing out of this movement represent new efforts to achieve gardens that are easier to maintain, simply because the plants that are chosen are those that flourish naturally in a given area rather than those that need coaxing and pampering.

The utility of this approach was brought home with great impact during the two-year drought of recent years in California. Gardeners suddenly discovered that their access to unlimited supplies of water was the only reason they were able to have such a diversity of plant material in their gardens. As the water literally dried up, so did many of the plants whose requirements were not in keeping with naturally available supplies. Countless gardeners stood by helplessly as they watched their hard-won lawns, annuals, perennials, and other ornamental plants wither in the heat and drought. This picture did not turn out to be as bleak as it seemed at the time: The plants that survived became the basic plant list for a whole

new form of gardening that extended to garden design as well. Even though the drought ended and water again became available for gardening, the lessons were not lost. Interested gardeners went on to create gardens that were adapted to the native conditions of the larger landscape regardless of the presence of imported water.

An eloquent spokesperson for this "new" approach is Russell Beatty, landscape architect and professor of landscape architecture at the University of California at Berkeley. In a series of articles published in *Pacific Horticulture,* Beatty outlined the folly of depending on a lawn as the focal point of a garden in an arid climate. He advocated a return to the original response to gardening in California, which was basically a Mediterranean style, featuring enclosed "patio gardens" where plants were limited to a well-adapted few, with those few creating the feeling of an oasis nonetheless. The first mission gardens in California, before the state was blanketed with an irrigation system, were basically gardens of this sort. The original gardeners of the era knew full well what it took subsequent gardeners two hundred years and a lack of water to figure out.

This approach has found a home in gardens across the United States, resulting in

Two very different variations on the same theme. Left: This house in the Northeast is set in an oak-maple forest, which has been altered by the selective removal of trees and the addition of the periwinkle ground cover. Shrubs are mountain laurel. Above: This New Orleans garden features plants that are well adapted to the area, and that have been allowed to grow in their own way. Landscape architect Christopher Friedrichs used ferns, dracaena, river birch, and banana to create this lush, tropical scene.

the popularization of such regional responses as the prairie gardens of the Midwest and the woodland gardens of the Eastern Seaboard.

Gradually, Beatty's approach has developed into a whole new school of thought regarding the creation of landscapes. At its most extreme, gardens are exact duplications of landscapes in the wild at various stages of their succession and rely *totally* on the use of native plants.

This type of landscaping, for all its apparent natural randomness, is the result of great sophistication, requiring considerable research and informed effort on the part of the gardener. Such gardens can be quite compelling and successful; however, the average gardener may not consider the results worth the effort and the time required for a completely natural garden to evolve as an easy maintenance alternative to the traditional garden.

The Modified Approach for Easy Maintenance

We can take our lead from proponents of natural landscapes with native plants but modify it to bring it more into line with our goal of easy maintenance gardening. If you want to make establishing a natural landscape a less demanding undertaking, you can relax your standards a bit and allow some well-chosen, nonnative plants in your garden. Many plants from climates similar to yours will actually outperform native plants. If you keep in mind that what you're after is a garden that basically grows by itself, your choices should include all willing participants.

Perhaps the easiest natural landscapes are created around dwellings in areas with distinct regional characteristics, such as seaside locations, forest lands, and foothills. In fact, homes in areas with unique natural landscapes are often designed to take advantage of the outstanding features of the existing landscape and require minimal enhancement from the gardener. This, of course, is provided that the gardener does not give in to an impulse to make the garden something that it is not. If you have an existing special landscape, count your blessings and learn to respect what's there. You will be rewarded for this discipline with a garden that is truly easy to maintain.

If you are trying to create a modified nat-

ural garden from bare ground, a situation facing many people who find themselves living in new developments and in urban settings where vestiges of native growth have all but disappeared, you will need to find out what the natural plant community is or was. One way to do this is to head out into the surrounding countryside to do a little fact finding. If the plants you see there are unfamiliar to you, take a few leaf specimens (as long as you're not foraging in protected lands!) to show to your local garden or nursery center for identification. As you gather specimens, look for the overall "style" of the countryside: configuration of rock outcroppings; the relationship of overhanging trees to shrubby undergrowth and grasses; the

Top: Another view of the house and landscape shown on page 41 left. Left: This natural scene was designed by Connecticut landscape architect A.E. Bye. Above: The stone pavers used for edging are set into the drive two feet deep, and at an angle, to prevent frost heave.

Above left: A third view of the house and garden shown on page 41 left and 42 top. Daylilies and daffodils are naturalized in beds of periwinkle under a canopy of oaks, beeches, and maples. The lawn is deliberately maintained "rough" to evoke the image of a meadow in a forest clearing. Above: The natural woods of beech, maple, and mountain laurel were carefully thinned to enhance the view beyond. Left: It takes an expert to tell which stones are natural and which were imported into the garden. The mixture of plants is as subtle. Native mountain laurel, maple, birch, and pine complement the introduced columbine and periwinkle.

nature of open areas, whether they are rocky, bare soil or covered with a thick layer of leaf litter. Should it appeal to you, pay special attention to creekside settings. These special microclimates abound in plants that exist only in the presence of shade and moisture. Creekside habitats are among the most attractive scenes to transplant to a private garden, and such success can be achieved with a minimum of effort.

Keep in mind that many native plants are poorly adapted to common garden conditions. In the wild, such plants are adapted to a very specific ecological niche, and success with them requires the gardener to re-create these niches with near precision—a most difficult task. Plants commonly available at nurseries, on the other hand, grow successfully in a comparatively wide range of environmental conditions, which is why they were selected for commercial nursery use to begin with. If, when you take your plant specimens into the nursery for identification, you discover that you have included several of these finicky plants, it is prudent and wise to ask for a closely related commercially available alternative. From the easy maintenance perspective, there is no good to be gained from a rigid approach to the creation of a natural landscape.

Benderboards separate the redwood chip mulch from the gravel walk. Automatic sprinkler in foreground.

Opposite page: Constructing edgings.
1. Wood beam or railroad ties edge gravel patio.
2. Raised concrete edging.
3. Flush concrete edging.
4. Staked wood form edging a brick patio.
5. Angled bricks set in mortar.
6. A 2 × 4 edging with submerged concrete curb.
7. Flush 2 × 4 edge.
8. Above-grade 2 × 4 edge.

WATERING SYSTEMS— BASICS AND VARIATIONS

No matter where you live, if you have plants, you have to water them. It's also true that many gardeners feel tied to their yard by a length of garden hose, especially during the summer season. It's not unusual for people who live in areas with warm summers and infrequent rains to feel trapped by the demands of a thirsty garden.

The information in this section takes up where the old-fashioned garden hose leaves off. There have been many advances in irrigation methods during the past few years, and several of these are now available to home gardeners.

Automated Sprinkler Systems

Automatic underground sprinkler systems have been in existence for over fifty years, but only in the last five years has the cost been substantially reduced. According to Dr. James R. Watson, Jr., Director of Agronomy for Toro Manufacturing: "New sprinkler heads with wider coverage and the use of plastic pipe—more effective and longer lasting than galvanized iron, brass, or copper—have brought systems within the reach of every homeowner."

Although the systems still require a sizable outlay, they can be considered an investment increasing the value of your property. Most commonly available systems average 60 to 80 cents per square foot. Factors affecting the cost one way or the other are: the number of trees and shrubs to be watered, the shape of your property, and the soil conditions.

Watson noted that "part of the investment in such a sprinkler system is returned through lower water bills." Most people assume that because an automatic sprinkler system keeps the grass greener, it uses more water. Actually, automatic sprinkler systems usually save water by supplying only the amount needed, and that at the proper time. If the system is well designed, it will deliver water only as fast as the soil can absorb it—like a gentle rain—so there is no loss from runoff.

One of the advantages of automatic lawn and yard watering is that it can be easily programmed for the early morning hours, ideally from 4:00 A.M. to 6:00 A.M. At that time water pressure from municipal systems is the highest, wind is minimal, and water loss by evaporation is negligible.

Homeowners with established landscapes are often concerned that their hard-won lawns will be destroyed by trenches and mounds of earth during an installation. New pipe-pulling and sodding equipment make such concerns groundless. If the work is to be done in relatively sandy and rock-free soil, the most efficient way to go is to use a pipe-pulling machine. Marks left by this equipment are hardly noticeable.

In heavy or rocky soil, it's best to use a sod-cutting machine (available at most rental yards) to strip the lawn where the trenches are to be dug. Once the trench is filled and the sod replaced, thin lines will be visible for only a few days before they completely disappear.

The installation of a sprinkler system is not beyond the range of the ambitious do-it-yourselfer. Even so, a novice should get all the information he or she can from a qualified dealer. If time is a consideration and cost is not, a professional installer can normally complete the average installation in one day.

When you plan your system, be sure to take into account trees, shrubs, and border plantings. Special sprinkler heads, which can save considerable time and energy, are available for just these situations.

Moisture Sensors. Whatever kind of sprinkler system you have, it can be more efficient if complemented with a moisture sensor. One of these new units almost gives a sprinkler system brain power. With a standard watering clock, in contrast, a sprinkler system is programmed to activate invariably at the same times, whether or not water is needed—even in the middle of a rainstorm. Water is never used in this illogical way when its application is controlled with a moisture sensor.

A moisture sensor is much like an electronic root. It is buried in the root zone, where it monitors moisture conditions. As soon as the soil is too dry, it signals the electric valve to open, thus automatically compensating for changing seasonal water needs.

If you have a timer governing your sprinkler system now, you can still use the electric valve in combination with the moisture sensor. A manual valve can be replaced by an electric one or easily converted by unscrewing the on-off control and replacing it with an electrical version.

Controllers. The heart of the automatic sprinkler system is the controller, and many models are available. Most allow for the adjustment of each sprinkler circuit in times ranging from a few minutes to more than an hour. This feature means that sprinklers covering areas with differing water needs can be programmed according to those needs.

There are two kinds of controllers: battery-powered controllers, which attach directly to the top of the valve actuator; and tensiometers, which operate in conjunction with an electric timer.

Electromechanical controllers are electric clocks with three control wheels. One

Before you begin digging up your yard, draw a plan of your proposed sprinkler system. The finished plan should show all the heads and valves connected by pipes. Also list all the parts you will need, including numbers and prices.

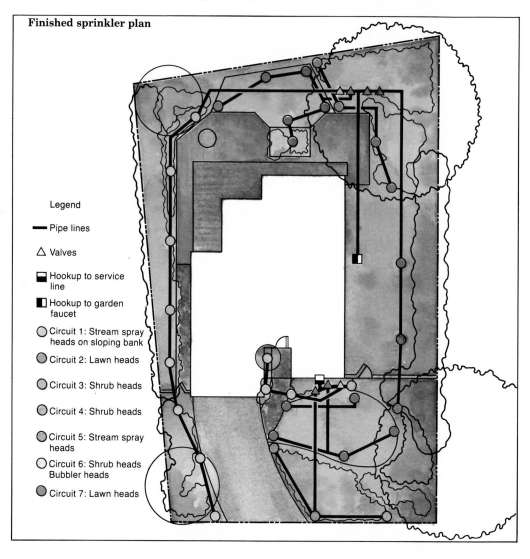

Finished sprinkler plan

Legend

— Pipe lines

△ Valves

▭ Hookup to service line

◼ Hookup to garden faucet

◯ Circuit 1: Stream spray heads on sloping bank

◯ Circuit 2: Lawn heads

◯ Circuit 3: Shrub heads

◯ Circuit 4: Shrub heads

◯ Circuit 5: Stream spray heads

◯ Circuit 6: Shrub heads Bubbler heads

◯ Circuit 7: Lawn heads

of these wheels governs the days the sprinkler goes on, usually out of a two-week cycle. A second wheel governs the time of day the sprinkler turns on, and the third wheel controls the length of time it is on.

Solid-state controllers have recently become available. These controllers look something like a calculator, with numbered buttons and a display screen. Solid-state controllers usually offer more flexibility in watering patterns than electromechanical controllers do.

The use of controllers for irrigation reduces the time spent watering to a few minutes a month spent changing the controller setting as the weather changes.

The advantage of tying a sensor to a timer in this manner is that you always know when the water will go on. The system is easily set to water during the optimum period (between 4:00 A.M. and 6:00 A.M.) every day. If your soil is slow to accept water, the timer can also be set to cycle on and off at short intervals. In this mode, the water comes on for ten minutes, then goes off for five minutes, giving the soil a chance to absorb the water. The on-off cycle repeats until the sensor indicates there is enough water. This system is particularly helpful for watering steep slopes or in other situations where excessive runoff is a problem.

If you are interested in installing an automatic sprinkler system yourself, check first at your local nursery or garden center to become familiar with the various systems available. Ortho's book *All About Landscaping* offers complete information on installation and can serve as a valuable guide.

Drip Systems

The idea of drip irrigation was born over forty years ago in the mind of Symcha Blass, an Israeli engineer. He happened to notice that a large tree near a leaky faucet grew more vigorously than other trees in the area watered by conventional means. With this clue he and other inventors eventually refined a system of watering that today consists basically of small, plastic irrigation tubes, the lateral lines, installed directly next to the plants to be watered. Holes, or "emitters," located at appropriate points along the lateral lines, deliver water to the plants slowly but steadily. The amount of water needed by the plant is supplied at a constant rate, an approach radically different from conventional irrigation methods, which provide quantities of water followed by periods of drought. Main lines and a "head," or control station, are the other parts of this system.

Emitters. Emitter models vary from the porous-wall types to the more complex, mechanical units that deliver water to a specific point. Emitters can reduce the flow of water to drips. Although some emitters are adjustable, the flow rate of most is fixed between ½ and 2 gallons per hour.

Lateral and Main Lines. Emitters are connected to lateral lines, usually made of plastic and relatively small in diameter—⅜–¾ inch. Lateral lines may cover long distances without losing pressure (avoiding a problem common to conventional irrigation systems) because the flow rates are slow. Even so, their installation should be as level as possible, particularly if the system uses less than 10 pounds of water pressure.

The main lines for drip systems, also plastic, can be installed above or below ground. The size of the main lines depends on the number of lateral lines and on the rate of water flow.

The "Head." At the "head," or control station, the water flow is measured and filtered, and the pressure is regulated. If an automatic time clock is to be part of the system, it is installed in the head.

Water used for drip must be free of sand and other particles, or the emitters will become plugged. To ensure water purity, sand or cartridge filters are used.

Left: A well-planned sprinkler system can be one of the biggest labor-saving devices in the garden, especially in areas that receive little summer rain. When combined with an automatic controller, shown above, the sprinkler system becomes truly automatic. This particular controller is the product of solid-state technology, and is programmed by pushing buttons, much like a small computer.

Drip systems may require reduction of water pressure, depending on the rate of flow from your tap. The pressure needed by the particular emitter you choose will be indicated by the manufacturer.

The Customized System. A research excursion to your local garden center will give you information on how to customize a drip system. Some of the most popular "extras" include fertilizer injectors, time clocks, and moisture sensors.

You can handle the fertilizing of your plants automatically while they are being irrigated—a definite boon in the easy maintenance garden—if you make a fertilizer injector part of your system. Nitrogen is often applied this way because it is readily available in a completely soluble, liquid form. Keep in mind, though, that any fertilizer material should be completely liquefied; otherwise, the risk that residue will clog the system is considerable. Be very wary too of using phosphorus fertilizers. The phosphate reacts with calcium in the water, forming a hard crust, which will work havoc on the system. In spite of these limitations, automatic fertilizing is a sophisticated technique especially popular with greenhouse growers who like the degree of control and freedom it gives them.

Time clocks, or controllers, are easy to add to the head. They can be set to initiate water applications ranging in duration from five minutes to twenty-four hours at any predetermined interval. The clocks are connected to electric valves, which control the water flow as necessary.

Moisture sensors can be used to activate drip systems. For a description of these units, see page 49.

Potential Problems. The most common problem with drip systems is plugged emitters. Even if the system is filtered correctly and the fertilizer carefully chosen, algae and mineral deposits often develop in the drip system lines between waterings. Once a month, check each emitter to be sure it is working. This takes about 10 or 15 minutes on a medium-sized yard. Check with the manufacturer for specific directions and cautions for correcting clogged systems.

The Advantages. Drip watering systems have proven advantages.

■ Water conservation. Water is applied only where it is needed, so less is used. There is virtually no runoff, and very little water is lost to evaporation. An important benefit of precise and limited watering is fewer weeds.

■ Effective fertilizing. Liquid fertilizers can be injected into the drip system and applied at the root zone where they do the most good. Less fertilizer is lost to overwatering and runoff.

■ Improved plant growth. Plants tend to grow more rapidly and are generally healthier because stress caused by alternate wet and dry cycles is practically eliminated.

■ Easy maintenance. The entire system is easily automated. Occasional spot checking for and cleaning of clogged emitters may be the only maintenance needed.

■ Flexibility. The system is not as carefully balanced as a sprinkler. New emitters or new laterals can be added or removed easily.

MULCH—THE GARDENER'S BEST FRIEND

To list all the good things a mulch does in the garden is to sound like a hawker selling snake oil: "Cures everything from lovesickness to rheumatism." But the claims for mulching are not inflated. For the gardener looking to lighten his or her work load, a mulch—a layer of organic matter spread a couple of inches thick over the surface of the soil—is nothing short of a miracle worker.

■ By insulating the top few inches of the soil from the sun's heat and by maintaining soil moisture up to the surface, a mulch gives the roots a free run in the richest layers of the soil.

■ A 2-inch layer of mulch will cut back on weeding chores significantly; 5 inches of mulch will eliminate them. Most weed seedlings won't be able to grow through it on their own stored food. Some perennial weeds will thrive in spite of the mulch, but they will definitely be easier to pull once they sprout through the surface.

■ Mulches slow down the evaporation of water from the upper 6–8 inches of soil, which means that the cultivated area will need less water. Tests show that merely shading the bare soil will reduce evaporation by as much as 30 percent, but a straw mulch, for example, will reduce evaporation by as much as 70 percent.

ORGANIC MULCHES

Bagasse
Light-colored residue of sugar cane after processing; clean and slow to decompose.

Bark
Usually fir; very long lasting and attractive. Eventual breakdown contributes much humus to soil. Use medium or coarse grades for mulch, fine for soil amendment.

Buckwheat hulls
Handsome dark-brown color and very fine textured; long lasting but subject to wind dispersal. Apply it to a depth of about 2 inches. Possibility of some odor during hot, humid weather.

Compost
Excellent mulch and soil conditioner usually made at home. Fully decomposed composts can be used under coarser mulches.

Corncobs
Most useful chopped into ½- to 1-inch particles. The sugar content stimulates beneficial soil organisms. Some additional nitrogen fertilizer is necessary.

Cottonseed hulls
May be too fine to resist blowing and washing; mixed with a heavier material, will make an excellent mulch.

Hay
An excellent and widely favored mulch. Use the type cut before seedheads were formed or risk introducing new weeds. Alfalfa or vetch hays decay fast and contribute considerable nitrogen to the soil.

Hops
Good mulch where available; brewery odor usually lasts at least a few weeks.

Lawn Clippings
Good if mixed with another, coarse mulch or allowed to dry before use. Don't use if lawn has been treated with weed killer; and don't use fresh clippings piled deeper than 1 inch (they'll mat and ferment).

Leaf mold
Available commercially, collected from woods, or made by composting your own supply of autumn leaves; beneficial to wild flowers and many other plants.

Leaves
Usually best if added to the compost pile and used in spring. Maple and similar soft leaves will mat otherwise. Oak leaves usually don't pack and are slightly acid, so they make an excellent azalea or rhododendron mulch.

Manure (strawy)
Good soil builder and source of nutrients; most often worked into the soil as an amendment rather than used as a mulch. It can burn plants if applied too heavily while fresh, and often carries weed seed or salts.

Mushroom compost
Good color and physical characteristics; decomposes quickly. High salt content is typical.

Peanut hulls
Good, nonpacking mulch but not especially good looking; should be fumigated before use to eliminate possibility of nematode infestation.

Pecan hulls
Good, long-lasting mulch where available.

Pine needles
Good and attractive mulch available wherever pine trees grow. The little acid they contain is beneficial to azaleas, rhododendrons.

Rice hulls
Good, long-lasting material; rather light and subject to winds. Try mixing with a denser material such as compost or grass clippings.

Sawdust
Very common mulch material in areas where readily available. Reports of toxic materials in sawdust have not been substantiated. For best results, use in layers and avoid sour sawdust that has fermented.

Seaweed
An excellent mulch that contains many minerals and other soil- and plant-benefiting elements; not attractive used around ornamental plantings unless shredded or composted.

Straw
Coarser than hay, a good general mulch, especially for winter protection. Do not use straw where it could be ignited. It is many times more flammable than hay. Straw frequently carries weed seed.

Tobacco stems
An attractive and effective mulch, usually available chopped; has insecticidal and repellent properties. Do not use it around bulbs or tomatoes because it may transmit mosaic disease.

MANUFACTURED AND INORGANIC MULCHING MATERIALS

Fiberglass matting
Effective, attractive, and useful mulch; readily permeable to air and water and blocks weed growth; useful for several seasons.

Marble chips
A very coarse slow-weathering form of limestone useful for maintaining proper pH in acid soil areas.

Microfoam
Available in ¼-inch-thick sheets, 6 feet wide, 250 feet long; excellent insulator used as blanket for winter protection.

Plastic film
Serves as an effective mulch by providing long-term control of some of the most tenacious weeds. Appearance can be improved by covering with a thin layer of organic mulch. Black plastic is usually preferred. Clear plastic allows the sun's warmth but also permits weed growth. Any color should be well perforated to allow water penetration, or a drip or soaking system should be used under the plastic.

Stone
Common where organic materials are scarce; available in a variety of colors to blend with surroundings. Use herbicide or plastic underneath to prevent weed growth. Stone holds the sun's heat in spring and fall and warms the soil. Stone bark is a manufactured stone resembling bark.

■ Mulches reduce soil erosion and compaction from heavy rains and irrigation water by baffling the water's fall, causing the water to seep slowly into the soil.

■ Mulches improve soil structure, which in turn improves plant growth. As microorganisms in the soil decompose the mulch, they secrete humus, the sticky substance that holds soil particles together. If the layer of mulch is maintained over several seasons, no cultivation of the soil will be necessary. And if you don't disturb the soil by overcultivating, the structure of the soil will slowly be transformed into an ideal state.

■ A mulch in the vegetable garden has unique benefits. When placed beneath unstaked tomatoes, summer squash, cucumbers, or strawberries, a mulch will lessen the loss of fruit through rot. A tomato that rests directly on damp soil is liable to rot from the action of soil bacteria. And even a thin layer of mulch will keep muddy splashes of rain water from starting rot in lettuce.

Mulching and Easy Maintenance

The easy maintenance gardener will be particularly interested in mulching for its effect on watering, weeding, and soil temperature.

Mulches and Water. Water applied to the garden—either by sprinkler or as rain—is lost in several ways: by runoff; by transpiration through the leaves of the plants; by draining through the soil; and by evaporation from the soil surface. For water to be lost by transpiration and drainage is normal, of course, and a mulch will not interfere with these processes. What a mulch can do, though, is reduce both runoff and evaporation, leaving more water available for plant use.

The effect of water falling on unprotected soil is the same as it would be if thousands of minute hammers hardened the soil surface by pounding away at it. Once the open surface of the soil is destroyed, its capacity to absorb water is quickly lost. The result is runoff and the eventual erosion of the topsoil. A layer of mulch absorbs the impact of the water as it drops and keeps the surface structure of the soil intact.

If a mulch is not used, water in the soil is drawn back by the sun to the surface and is lost through evaporation. A mulch acts

as a one-way door, allowing water to enter the soil but blocking its return. A 2-inch layer of mulch can reduce seasonal evaporation from the soil by as much as 70 percent, and that can represent a considerable savings in the time and money spent on watering. It's not unusual for the time a vegetable or flower bed can go between waterings to double when a mulch is used.

Mulches and Soil Temperature. Both organic and manufactured mulches have a dramatic effect on soil temperatures, a consideration in areas with extremes in climate. A 3-inch layer of organic mulch can keep the top 8 inches of soil as much as 10 degrees cooler than unmulched soil. Light-colored manufactured mulches reflect the sun and also cool the soil. A cooling effect is important in climates with hot weather because the roots of many plants cannot live in soil temperatures above 100 degrees Fahrenheit.

Mulches of all varieties also help to mod-

A thick layer of organic mulch, such as the straw shown above in a bed of strawberries, can practically work miracles in any garden. Mulching is one of the best practices a person can do to limit the amount of work a garden requires.

ify soil temperatures at the opposite end of the thermometer. In areas where a season-long snow mulch is not a certainty, a winter mulch can keep the soil frozen solid all winter. This prevents the alternate freezing and thawing so damaging to bulbs, recently planted trees and shrubs, and shallow-rooted perennials.

The time to apply a winter mulch is *after* the ground has completely frozen. If put down too early, the mulch may promote new growth that will be killed later by the cold.

The best winter mulch is a material that will not pack down, blocking air to the soil. The mulch should be applied 3–4 inches thick.

Don't be too eager to remove the mulch in spring. Loosen it only during the first warm days of spring. Soil heated too early will promote growth that can be caught by a late frost.

Mulches and Weed Control. Mulches are one of the most practical and effective methods of weed control in the garden, a valuable benefit for the easy maintenance gardener. The simple act of shading the soil prevents many seeds from germinating. Those that do get started are much easier to pull from a loose mulch than from hard soil.

How thick should you apply a mulch for effective weed control? The answer depends both on the mulch and on the types of weeds you normally have problems with. A 2-inch layer of wood chips will be an effective barrier to most annual weeds, but most tough perennial weeds such as Bermuda grass, nutgrass, and oxalis will shoot right through even a 4-inch layer of mulch.

Black plastic will keep perennial weeds from being a problem. Even those seeds that germinate under it will wither and die from lack of sunlight. Gardeners plagued with perennial weeds often put down a layer of black plastic film and cover it with a couple of inches of organic mulch, stones, gravel, or other decorative material.

Bermuda grass is a very persistent weed, and it will eventually work its way around to the edges of a plastic mulch in search of sunlight. The best control in this situation is to spot spray the Bermuda grass that comes up past the plastic with a herbicide such as dalapon or gylphosate. Check at your nursery or garden center for products containing those active ingredients.

PLANTING TREES AND SHRUBS

Although the following instructions for planting trees and shrubs may seem a little old-fashioned and finicky, there is no question that any plant that is correctly planted will have a much better chance at being an easy maintenance plant than one that is carelessly plopped in the ground.

If a tree or shrub gets off to a good start by being well planted, it can start growing right away, without having to struggle for existence in its new home. Any plant that does not thrive is a disappointment to its owners and will probably need plenty of attention if the original planting mistakes are to be corrected (provided they can be). And a plant that has been poorly planted is subject to attack from pests and diseases, which

This gardener is preparing to plant a balled and burlapped nandina.

means more work for the owners and less chance for survival for the plant.

The best techniques for planting shrubs and other plants are the techniques that have been used throughout the centuries. The few modifications that we present are the result of experimentation by nursery personnel and researchers.

Most trees and shrubs adapt well to the large middle range of native soils available to most gardeners. But because nursery plants are grown in a light-weight, porous growing medium formulated to keep the plants healthy while they are in their containers, they have to go through a period of transition when they are planted in garden soil. Some plant experts feel that this transition is eased if transition soil is used. Simply, before you replace the soil from the planting hole, you amend it to approximate the container soil.

Recent research has turned up an unexpected finding. Although plants started out in transition soil thrive better and grow faster at first than those planted in unamended backfill soil, after a couple of years they lose their edge, becoming less healthy. Eventually their roots must penetrate the native soil, and the research indicates that doing so sooner rather than later may actually establish a stronger root system.

If you have a problem soil, chances are that your best gardening success will come from selecting plants that are particularly adapted to that soil. Otherwise, your plants will probably do well using either method of planting.

The Planting Steps

If you carefully follow the planting steps outlined here, success is practically guaranteed, and you will be enjoying superintending a healthy, growing garden rather than watching over a hospital ward. The steps described are for shrubs and trees bought in containers, but the steps for planting balled and burlapped plants are essentially the same.

Plant at the Right Time. Early spring and early fall have always been recommended as the ideal times for planting shrubs and trees. Actually, this traditional advice may be a bit strict. You can plant at any time, with two limitations. Don't plant before the soil is workable. If you can't use a spade or cultivator easily, wait until the soil dries out a little. It is also not a good idea to plant immediately preceding a period that will cause the plant climate-related stress. Late spring and late fall are usually times when the approaching heat or cold will stress newly established plants.

Dig the Hole. Dig the planting hole approximately twice as wide and either to the same depth as the rootball or 1 inch shallower. Plants have a tendency to sink after they have been planted, so if the hole is dug deeper than the original rootball, the plant may suffer in time from crown and root rot. The rootball should be resting on firm, undisturbed soil.

Amend the Backfill Soil (Optional). If you are going to prepare a transition soil, this is the time to do it. The soil that you take from the hole is called *backfill soil.* Keep the backfill in one pile and make a rough estimate of its volume. Then add an organic soil amendment to the pile, one that decomposes slowly. The proportion of soil conditioner to backfill soil is flexible, but approximately 25 percent of the final mix should be conditioner.

Take the Plant out of the Container. Plants grown in plastic containers will slip out easily, especially if the rootball is damp. Be careful with the rootball, however. If you break it trying to get it out of the container, you may permanently damage the root system. If the container is a straight-sided metal can and you are going to plant the shrub the same day you buy it, have the can cut at the nursery. Cut the can at home just before planting (with a large pair of tin snips or a can cutter) if the planting is going to be delayed even for a day or two.

Place in the Hole. Before putting the plant in the hole, check the rootball. Cut or pull away any circled, matted, or tangled roots so that they radiate out from the rootball. Matted roots often stay that way, not venturing into the surrounding soil. Shorten the roots to the width of the planting hole so they will not be bent when planting. To compensate for damaged or cut roots, lightly trim the top of the plant. Check the rootball depth in relation to the planting hole depth, and in it goes.

If proper steps are taken in planting a tree or shrub, the maintenance will be minimized.
1. Dig the hole and test depth and width before removing the plant from the container.
2. If you choose to amend the backfill, do it now.
3. Add nutrients according to directions and mix into the soil.
4. Remove the plant from the container.
5. Cut or prune away any matted or tangled roots.
6. Place plant in the hole and fill in the soil.
7. Build a basin for watering.
8. Stake if necessary and water thoroughly.

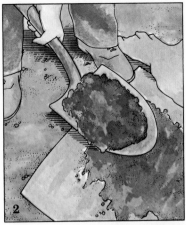

Fill the Hole. Fill the hole with backfill soil to the level of the surrounding soil.

Build a Basin. Build a shallow basin around the plant so that irrigation water will be concentrated in the area where it is most needed. Be sure to build it so that the water drains away from the stem of the plant. Thoroughly water the soil around the root zone. Apply water until the soil is loose and muddy. Gently jiggle the plant until it is positioned exactly as you want it. This action will eliminate any remaining air pockets. Check again to be sure water drains away from the stem of the plant. Use the basin for primary watering until some roots have had a chance to expand into the surrounding soil—usually in about six weeks. If dry weather conditions require continued irrigation, enlarge the basin at the six-week point (or whenever the roots have become established). If you live in an area with sufficient summer rain or if you have installed another irrigation system, you can now break down the basin.

Stake If Necessary. Recent tests have shown that some back-and-forth movement of the tops of plants actually results in faster and better-quality growth. The only reasons to stake a newly planted tree or shrub are if the plant is extremely top heavy or if it is planted in an area of high winds. If a stake is necessary, place it on the side of prevailing winds. You can also use two stakes, one on either side of the plant, and tie them loosely for support with something that will not damage the surface of the stem, such as an old bicycle inner tube.

Check ties often to make sure that they are not biting into the growing plant. Stakes can be removed after the plant is securely rooted in its new location, usually after the first year.

Water. Monitor the plant to see how much water it requires. If a newly planted tree or shrub wilts during the hottest part of the day, the rootball is not getting enough water even though the surrounding soil may appear wet. Even if it rains or if the plant is in the path of a sprinkler, you may need to water it by hand two or three times a week for the first few weeks if the soil is dry. But do not overwater—too much water is as harmful as too little.

Dry Fertilizer Spreaders

There are two types of dry fertilizer spreaders: broadcast spreaders and drop spreaders. Hand-held broadcast spreaders are the ones most commonly used by noncommercial gardeners; they are excellent for small- to medium-size lawns. Wheeled broadcast spreaders work on the same principle as the hand-held models, but they are designed to cover a large area quickly and are most effective on flat, large lawns. The drop spreader is not as fast as the broadcast spreader, but it gives a more even distribution.

Liquid Fertilizer Application

For those who prefer to use a liquid fertilizer over large lawn or ground cover areas, or who like to foliar feed in early spring, the hose-end sprayer is the device of choice. The basic version consists of a glass or plastic jar suspended beneath a nozzle that attaches to the end of a hose. The jar contains the correctly diluted spray; the nozzle mixes precise amounts of the dilution with the stream of water. Most hose-ends require you to premix concentrate and water in the jar for further dilution in the water stream. Others are designed so that blending and dilution are done in the spraying head. The dilution ratio of product to water is controlled by a dial on the head. Most of these heads can attach directly to the original product bottle. All that you need to do after the application is to clean the nozzle head. If you have only a few indoor plants or containers outdoors, the easiest method of application is to use a watering can, diluting the fertilizing solution with water.

CULTIVATING

The yearly tilling of the soil in farms and gardens has been an accepted practice for as long as people have gardened. More tools and equipment are devoted to cultivating soil than perhaps to any other gardening chore. In most modern-size gardens, the emphasis may be misplaced.

Current research now indicates that soil can be overcultivated, destroying its structure to the point where plant growth is inhibited rather than enhanced. To create a garden soil that needs little or no cultivation requires the advance preparation outlined on pages 45 and 46 and the yearly addition of an organic mulch in spring. Using this system, all that is necessary is to lightly incorporate last year's mulch into the top layer of the soil before applying another layer in spring.

Power cultivators, such as electric- and gas-powered cultivators or rotary tillers, are indispensable when it comes to doing the initial soil preparation for vegetable gardens, lawn and ground cover plots, and flower and shrub borders. They can do in minutes what normally takes hours with a shovel or hand cultivator. The power cultivators are suited for use in gardens of a quarter acre or less; the rotary tillers for larger grounds. Once the garden has been installed and mulching has become a regular practice, all that's needed to work the soil is a long-handled cultivator or a steel garden rake.

CONTROLLING WEEDS

Weeds and gardening go hand in hand. Even the smallest gardens have their fair share of weeds during one season or another. The time-honored and most laborious method of dealing with weeds is to pull them out by hand. Other methods for controlling weeds are to use a hoe or a specially designed weeder, still removing the weeds with physical labor, or to use chemical products designed to kill a wide range of weeds or just one weed in particular. Perhaps the easiest method of all is to prevent weeds from growing in the first place by using a pre-emergent weed killer, a mulch, or a combination of both. What you choose will depend in part on where the weeds occur in the garden. One thing to remember is that the longer you wait after the weeds first appear, the bigger your job will be, no matter what method you use. The important thing is that weeds be eliminated before they mature, flower, and scatter seeds for next year's crop.

Controlling Weeds in Bare Ground

If you have an area in your garden that is unplanted but that needs to be kept free of weeds (for fire control or aesthetics), the efficiency of using chemicals is undeniable. Systemics are among the most effective chemical herbicides (they are actually absorbed by the plant through the leaves and into the roots, giving a complete kill) and are best applied when weeds are actively growing. The more leaf surface that is exposed and available to absorb the chemical, the more effective the application will be. If you are going to apply a systemic weed killer,

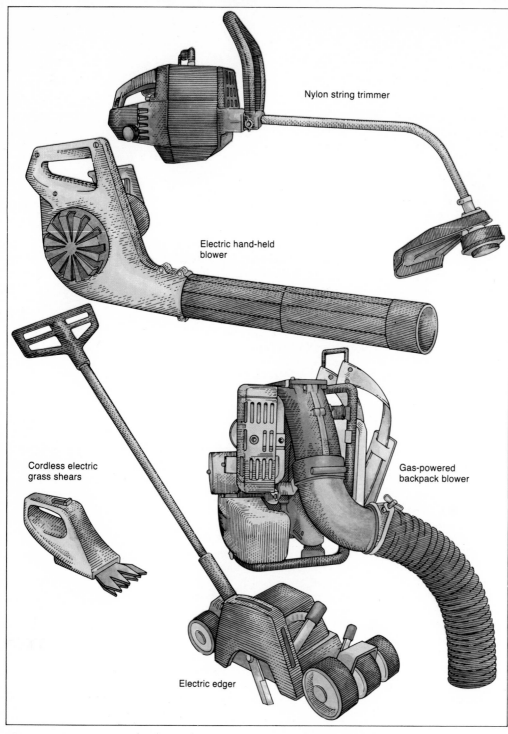

Nylon string trimmer

Electric hand-held blower

Cordless electric grass shears

Gas-powered backpack blower

Electric edger

Choose power tools that fit the major maintenance tasks your garden presents. Here are some of the most useful. The nylon-string trimmer can be used for many jobs (see page 67). Hand-held or backpack blowers are favorite time-saving tools for many gardeners (see page 68). And hand-held and push-type edgers cut down on the tedious task of trimming and edging (see page 67).

then, don't mow the weeds down first. A nonselective weed killer will kill all forms of vegetation whether they be broad-leafed or grassy. As with any chemical products, read and follow all label directions to the letter. Many products have an optimum range of temperatures for effectiveness. Failure to follow directions may make repeated applications necessary, adding both time and expense to the job. Most chemical weed control products are applied with a hose-end sprayer.

Mechanical elimination of weeds re-quires considerable work, especially if the area involved is large. The job is difficult and not as thorough as with chemical weed killers. Tools for weeding include hoes, scythes, and variations of both that simply knock the tops off the weeds. Also available are smaller, pronged hand tools designed to pull the roots out of the ground. For mechanical elimination of weeds, the action hoe, pictured on page 61, is perhaps the best choice of all the hoes. Its blade moves about half an inch each way when it's either pushed or pulled. This slight movement adjusts the blade angle so that it cuts down at the roots of weeds. Another device that's very effective is the scythelike jungle knife, a long (about 30 inches) tool with a blade sharpened on both edges to cut in both directions as you swing it back and forth. The jungle knife can be controlled for use close to trees and fences as well as over large, open areas. This tool is pictured on page 61.

Once the area is free of weeds, you should take steps to keep it that way by applying a pre-emergent weed killer or covering the soil with black plastic or a thick (3–4 inches) layer of organic mulch.

Controlling Weeds in Shrubs and Flower Beds

If the undesired plants are growing among desired ornamental plants, such as shrubs, perennials, or ground covers, the job of eliminating them becomes more complicated. Many gardeners simply remove the weeds by hand or use one of the tools we have mentioned, being careful not to disturb the roots of the desired plants.

If you prefer to use a chemical weed killer in this situation, you should be sure of two things: (1) that you have the right chemical for the job; and (2) that you apply it carefully to avoid having it drift onto desirable plants. Early mornings and evenings, when the wind is still, are the best times for this type of spraying. If you want to avoid new crops of weeds, once the area is clean—whether it be cultivated or bare ground—apply a pre-emergent weed killer or a thick layer of organic mulch.

Controlling Weeds in Lawns and Ground Covers

With the exception of dichondra, virtually all lawns are composed of one type of grass or another. Among the most common weeds in grass lawns are broad-leafed weeds. Broad-leafed weed killers eliminate the weeds without harming the grass. If you have a dichondra lawn, be sure to use only those products specially formulated for them; otherwise you will kill your dichondra lawn at the same time that you kill your weeds. Several infamous grassy weeds, such as crabgrass, annual bluegrass, and Dallis grass, can invade a lawn and require products specially formulated to kill them alone. If you've had a problem with these or other grassy weeds, timing the chemical appli-

cation is of critical importance. Crabgrass, for instance, can be completely eradicated but only by following a rather strict program. Existing crabgrass should be controlled in early spring, using a specialty product every seven to ten days until all traces are gone. Seeds of the crabgrass may still be present in the soil and should be kept from germinating in early spring. If you wait until summer, when patches of crabgrass are large and tough, the difficulty of the job will be greatly multiplied.

If the area that you plan to plant in a ground cover is presently host to perennial weeds, such as quackgrass, Bermuda grass, milkweed, or bindweed, the soil should be fumigated after it has been cultivated but before it is planted. Some landscape and pest-control companies offer this service. Fumigation is an exacting and difficult procedure and should be done with care and restraint. The first year a ground cover is planted is when most weed problems occur.

Once a ground cover is planted, a generous application of organic mulch (3–5 inches thick) will stop many of the most troublesome annual weeds and make it easier to pull out the ones that do sprout. If you don't intend to add a mulch and the area is free of weeds, there are several pre-emergent weed killers that can be used without harming the new ground cover. Most give control for six–twelve months. If you have broad-leafed weeds in a broad-leafed ground cover, remember to choose the product carefully to avoid killing your ground cover.

Once a ground cover planting is mature, the cover is usually so thick that weeds are not a problem. The ground cover itself inhibits seeds from sprouting.

CONTROLLING PESTS AND DISEASES

Gardeners who are on familiar terms with the plants in their gardens are the ones who have the fewest problems with pests and diseases. With a daily stroll in the garden, you can hold potential problems to a minimum just by keeping your eyes open for anything irregular: a chewed leaf, a disfigured bud, stunted foliage, a small patch of mildew or rust on a leaf, and so on.

If you take action at the first sign of attack, less damage is likely, and you'll also minimize the need for chemical controls. You can avoid problems by taking these steps:

Keep old leaves picked up; they often harbor disease organisms and are hiding places for snails, slugs, and damaging insects.

Remove and destroy any diseased leaves, flowers, or fruits. Do not put them on the compost pile. Disease spores can live from one season to the next.

Clean up thoroughly before winter sets in. Remove any debris and other likely homes for overwintering insects and diseases.

If the problem has gotten out of hand, there are many products available to help gardeners and plants alike. If your garden is small, most pesticides are available premixed in spray cans, which simplifies the whole procedure, eliminating the need for mixing, using a hose-end sprayer, and disposing of excess material. For larger areas, you'll need a hose-end sprayer or a tank sprayer. It's very important that you know what the plant is and what the pest is. As with all garden chemicals, read and follow all label directions carefully.

With all pesticides the application is at least half the battle. You must be sure to adequately cover the pests and their hiding places as the label directs. Never spray grass or any plant that is suffering from lack of moisture. Water deeply and thoroughly a few days before spraying. Wait a day or two after a period of strong wind so moisture lost from leaves can be replaced—leaves should be turgid. Never spray when bark or leaves are wet from dew, rain, or sprinkling—the spray will lose much of its effectiveness.

PRUNING

If you are in the planning stages of a garden, there are several things you can do to minimize the amount of pruning that will ultimately be required. Whenever possible, favor compact varieties of plants whose natural growth habit requires little pruning maintenance. Many compact varieties of old favorites, such as raphiolepis, holly, junipers, and pittosporum are currently available. When making choices for plants, as in looking through the *Plant Selection Guide,* make special note of the ultimate height and width of a plant. If you allow sufficient room for a plant to grow naturally, little corrective pruning will be needed. You won't be trying to keep the plant smaller than it wants to be. And the plants can achieve their natural forms, allowing you to avoid having

a collection of pruned geometric shapes, a situation common to some long-established gardens. For example, the English laurel, when given its own growth pattern, can reach heights of 30 feet with an equal width. Unfortunately, this plant is commonly used as a shrub in smaller gardens, where constant pruning is necessary to keep it in scale. A smaller substitute for the English laurel is the Japanese privet (*Ligustrum japonicum*), which has a dense, compact habit to 10 feet high and slightly less wide.

Part of allowing plants enough space for their natural growth is not to overplant in the first place. Although we know there is always the temptation to create an "instant" garden by planting quantities of plants, in the long run you will save considerable expense and time if you can keep in mind your ultimate goal, a beautiful garden that requires a minimum of maintenance. Overplanted gardens quickly result in maintenance nightmares.

Pruning Tools

If your pruning chores are not such that you want to call in professionals, you will have to have some pruning tools. Pruning tools are available in a variety of styles, each designed to do a specific type of pruning. The most important thing to remember when approaching a pruning task is to use an appropriate tool. As far as the labor of pruning goes, the mistake most frequently made is to try to prune large limbs with small tools. There are a number of consequences to doing a job this way. It takes you much longer than it should, the limb or branch is likely to be injured because you can't get a clean cut, you run the risk of damaging the tool you are using, and you reinforce your resolve never to touch shears again.

Another commonly made error that increases the difficulty of the task is buying tools with a grip that doesn't fit your hands. It seems a small point, but you will find the work much less tiring if you choose tools with grips that don't spring open wider than your hand.

Various hand pruners and loppers, their larger, more powerful, long-handled cousins, can be used to tackle branches up to 2 inches in diameter. For branches thicker than this, you will need a pruning saw. The standard pruning saw (illustrated on page 61) is curved, and the teeth are angled back,

which means that the cutting action occurs with the pull. The curve automatically forces the teeth into the cut.

The pole pruner (see page 61) is a recent development in pruning technology. All models work very simply, on the same principle, for branches up to 1½ inches in diameter. To use the pole pruner, slip the hook over the branch where the cut is to be made. Put pressure on the hook by pulling the pole toward you and then make the cut by pulling the rope (or lever). You can keep the tree clear as you work by removing cut branches with the hook. The advantage of the pole pruner is that it eliminates the need for a ladder—though no one has yet figured out how to avoid getting a crick in your neck if you use one for any length of time.

As you probably realize, the actual mechanics of pruning are somewhat involved owing to the different requirements of different plants; and in all fairness we cannot give proper attention to pruning details in this limited space. For the complete story, see Ortho's book *All About Pruning*.

TRIMMING AND EDGING

The difference between trimming and edging is between cutting vertically and cutting horizontally. *To trim* is to cut horizontally around trees, fences, and other obstructions in the lawn. *To edge* is to cut vertically, keeping the edges of the lawn next to walks, driveways, and planting beds neat and orderly. Some type of trimming is frequently necessary after mowing to give a lawn a manicured look. Trimming is a laborious task, adding significantly to the amount of time it takes to maintain a lawn. By avoiding any obstructions in the lawn and with appropriate edging material appropriately placed, you can avoid the necessity of trimming altogether. If this is not possible, consider the merits of a nylon string trimmer or cordless electric grass shears. All you need to do is point the shears in the right direction and turn on the switch. They will cut for thirty–forty minutes at a time and can be fully recharged in twenty-four hours. They are most effective for trimming grass and very light weeds.

Also worthwhile are border and lawn shears designed to let you stand up while you do a chore usually requiring kneeling or stooping. Such shears, pictured on page 61, will save you sore knees and a tired back.

As we discussed on pages 47 and 48, there are steps you can take in the planning stage that will all but eliminate edging chores. If, however, your garden does require edging, an electric edger such as the one pictured on page 64 will pare the job down to a reasonable size.

The Nylon-String Trimmer
Relatively new and appropriate for small lawns and sloped lawns are the nylon-string trimmers. Nylon-string trimmers are truly multiuse garden tools that can be used as small lawn mowers, trimmers, edgers, and weed cutters. They are lightweight, easy to use, and especially effective for trimming lawns, ground covers, or other vegetation growing next to fences, walls, or tree trunks. The design of the trimmer allows close-up trimming without damaging adjoining surfaces and relieves much of the tedium associated with doing the job by hand.

The nylon-string trimmer—along with the power mower and the rotary tiller—ranks right at the top of the list of all-time major time savers. It can accomplish in half an hour or less a grass- or weed-trimming job that would take half a day by hand.

This Portland, Oregon garden, designed by Barbara Fealy, features a well-edged lawn, azaleas, rhododendrons, and irises under the shade of oaks and pines. Easy maintenance points include large areas of gravel paths, benderboard edging set low enough so a mower can be run over it, and liberal use of bark mulch to discourage weeds in beds.

The trimmer cuts by the rapid whirling action of a motor-driven nylon string. This method has a great advantage over such hand tools as grass whips or sickles: You can cut right against walls. When the flexible nylon filament strikes an obstruction, it does not break but merely wears away; then more nylon can be fed out.

Nylon-string trimmers are available in a variety of models, both electric- and gas-powered. What you use depends on the jobs you have in mind, but be sure to get one that has a semiautomatic or automatic feed system for the nylon filament. You will find this option invaluable if you are working in dense weeds that quickly wear away the nylon.

GARDEN CLEAN-UP

Picking up and disposing of garden debris has become an even more significant task in the many communities that have banned the burning of garden refuse.

Gardeners with mature deciduous trees know full well the scope of the chore. If burning is no longer an alternative, something must be done on a regular basis to avoid a massive pile up of debris, which seems to accumulate at a surprisingly rapid rate. Some sweeping, pruning, and raking, done in a fit of morning energy, can produce a good-size quantity of material to be disposed of. Short of having your own shredder and compost pile, the only realistic solution is to bag the material and have it hauled away or take it to the dump yourself.

The advent of the large, heavy duty plastic bag and several devices for holding it either upright or open is good news to easy maintenance gardeners. Two particular devices recommend themselves: the wheeled bag holder, and the Ring-Dang-Do, both pictured on page 60.

Sweepers and Blowers

If getting the debris into one place is a problem, you may want something besides the standard large garden rake or pushbroom. The push-type lawn sweeper is one option. If you have a medium- to large-size yard dotted with deciduous trees, a lawn sweeper (see page 60) will make your life easier during fall cleanup (and at other times too if your sweeper will also pick up clippings).

Essentially, a sweeper is a set of four to six rows of brushes attached to an axle. The brushes catch the leaves and throw them into the rear collecting bag.

Sweepers work best on smooth, level lawns. They operate close to the ground, so any irregularities can cause problems. Where the ground begins to rise, the sweeper's front end may dig into it; in a depression, the brushes will skip leaves.

One of the best time-saving all-season power tools is the power blower, one type of which is pictured on page 64. In winter, it can be used to remove light snow from cars and walkways. During the rest of the year, it can be used to blow water from tennis courts, walkways around swimming pools, and rain gutters; and to blow both wet and dry leaves into piles or wind rows for bagging or mulching. One landscaper declares that the blower is his single most valuable piece of equipment; it saves more time in commercial maintenance than any other tool.

Blowers come with either electric- or gas-powered engines. The electric blower is limited by the length of the cord and the possibility of becoming entangled in shrubbery, but it has the advantages of instant power, relative quietness, and no fussing with fuel mixing or engine maintenance. However, electric blowers offer a smaller range of power options than do gas-powered blowers.

Gas-powered blowers range from small hand-held or backpack models to the wheeled models that are used for large estates or small orchards. Their main advantage is that they allow unrestricted movement.

To determine what type of blower you need, consider: How much of the year will you need it for? How large is the area you want to cover? What is the weight of the debris to be blown? And what size and weight equipment can you use comfortably?

The Importance of Timing

You could have a storage shed full of the best tools, equipment, and garden products, but if you didn't know when to use them, they probably wouldn't do you much good. One of the most important aspects of saving work in the garden is preventing certain problems before they appear, and ridding the garden of others while they are still small. Both preventive and early-stage remedial measures need to be taken at the right time for them to be effective. Timing is what the following section is all about.

SEASONAL GUIDE TO EASY MAINTENANCE

In this guide we have arranged gardening chores by season. The intent in organizing them this way is not so much to give you a list to follow chore by chore as it is to remind you that certain conditions are far easier to prevent than to take care of once they become a problem. Timing is perhaps the most important aspect of any preventive measure. A little maintenance performed at the right time will save you much work in the long run. You will be busiest in spring and fall, the seasons when gardens demand the most maintenance. Summer and winter are for enjoyment and rest, respectively—at least as far as gardening goes.

For garden maintenance, the spring season is divided into early spring and late spring. *Early spring* means there's still a chance of a frost or two; *late spring* means after the last frost. That seemingly simple distinction makes a big difference with many garden activities.

Early Spring

Working with the soil. If you didn't work the soil last fall, now is the time to do it, before weeds have a chance to take over. Spread a 2- to 3-inch layer of organic material such as compost, well-rotted manure, or ground bark over the surface and work it into the soil to a depth of 6 inches using a spade or rototiller. The object is to break up the soil and to incorporate the organic material into the soil as thoroughly as possible. A 1- to 2-inch layer of organic mulch spread over the top of the soil will keep new weeds from sprouting.

Preparing to install a lawn. If you are planning to install a spring lawn, the soil can be prepared as soon as it dries out enough to be workable. Prepare the soil as described above, but omit the final layer of mulch. The deeper the soil is worked, the less maintenance will be needed in the future. Many experts recommend a depth of 12 inches. In soil prepared to this depth the grass can develop a deep, strong root system, better able to withstand both drought and disease and insect attacks. Wait until late spring to actually seed the lawn. For more complete instructions for preparing soil for lawns and other ground covers, see pages 45–46. If your warm-season grass lawn is already in place, fertilize it now with a product containing quick-acting nitrogen.

Spraying for insects. While plants are still fully dormant, oil-based sprays (dormant sprays) can be used to eliminate many overwintering insects. Once plants break dormancy, you should switch to an insecticide that will not harm tender new growth.

Transplanting. This is also the best time to move plants from one spot in the garden to another. Fully dormant plants are far less easily shocked than those already started on spring growth.

Checking equipment and tools. Before the season begins in earnest, take the time to check over garden equipment and tools, cleaning and sharpening them if necessary. You may find it useful to consult the Ortho book *How to Select, Use & Maintain Garden Equipment.* It gives very specific and thorough advice on care of all garden equipment.

Late Spring

Fertilizing. In planning when to fertilize plants, a good general rule to follow is to apply fertilizer only when plants are growing, not when they are dormant. (The exception is fertilizing flowering and fruiting plants with a fertilizer that does not contain any nitrogen, such as an 0-10-10 formulation.) Food energy stored in plants through the winter begins to be released in the warmer days of late spring; and it is during this period that most plants appreciate an application of a fast-acting fertilizer.

Fertilizer applied too early may encourage new, tender growth, which can be destroyed by end-season frosts. Plants assaulted in this way are stunted for the rest of the season.

Lawn repair. Lawns require special attention during late spring. A bare patch of lawn is an invitation to weeds; so repair bare spots with seed or sod now. If you are going to use seed, be sure to buy the same variety as the original lawn. Scratch the bare spot lightly with a small cultivator and press the seed into the soil with your hand or foot. An easier, instant even, solution is to replace the bare spot with a piece of sod. Use a sharp knife to remove the section of dead lawn. Cut a piece of sod the same size as the hole and press it into place.

Lawn rejuvenation. If your lawn is in need of an overall rejuvenation, you will have to aerate the soil (using an aerator, which extracts plugs of soil) and dethatch the grass before applying fertilizer.

Fertilizing lawns. Most lawns should receive two fertilizer applications in spring. Follow the manufacturer's instructions for rates of application.

Weed control for lawns. You can end your problems with crabgrass with an application of a pre-emergent herbicide. Used correctly, pre-emergent herbicides are very effective. Be sure to read the instructions carefully for timing dates. (For the complete story on lawn care, see the Ortho book *All About Lawns.*) Other lawn weeds can be prevented by mowing at the right height, fertilizing adequately, and watering properly. A vigorous, well-fed lawn will crowd out most weeds.

If weeds do become a problem in your lawn, you can either take them out by hand or kill them chemically using a product specially formulated to take care of those particular weeds.

Herbicides intended for use on home lawns are formulated according to weed type: broad-leafed or grassy. Pick a herbicide, and then find out how to use it: the time to apply it, the correct application rate and method, and follow-up recommendations. Spray right and you'll need to spray less.

There are two kinds of herbicides: the pre-emergent group and the post-emergent group. Pre-emergent herbicides are effective against germinating seeds and stop them before the plant emerges from the soil. Timing is the key to their success, but by using the right product at the right time you can stop even crabgrass—that most tenacious of weeds—from appearing in your lawn.

Post-emergent herbicides are the more conventional products. They will eliminate existing weeds but have no effect on weed seeds.

Watering. Watering adequately will also help to avoid problems. To keep grass roots growing deeply, the soil should be moistened to a depth of 6–8 inches, which means 1–2 inches of water delivered over the lawn surface. Depending on the weather and the soil type, the average lawn will deplete this amount of water in about a week. To tell if the water has gone deep enough, wait twelve hours and check with a soil sampler (available at garden supply centers) or simply poke a screwdriver in the ground. If it penetrates about 6 inches without much resistance, the lawn is usually wet enough. Water should be applied as uniformly as possible and no faster than the soil can absorb it. If there is runoff, divide your watering into timed intervals. Sprinkle until the soil can't take more; then stop for twenty or thirty minutes to allow for absorption. Continue this pattern until enough water has been applied. Many gardeners feel that mornings are close to the ideal time to water. The lawn has a chance to dry out during the day rather than staying soggy throughout the night. Evaporation caused by wind and sun are minimized, and sprinkler patterns are not disrupted by wind.

Pruning roses. The time to prune roses is after the last heavy frost, when the damage done by winter can be seen and removed. Remove dead canes as well as some of the oldest canes. Leave three to five canes that face outward, forming a vase shape. Pruning cuts should be sealed with a pruning paint to protect the plants against attacks.

Other rose care. Add a 1–2-inch layer of organic mulch to the rose bed to reduce watering needs later in the season and to prevent weeds from sprouting. Start your fertilization and disease and insect control program now. You can simplify your rose maintenance program by using one of the combination rose care products. Some of these products feed, weed, and protect the plants from chewing insects— all with one application. Check for these products at your garden center. Read and follow all label directions.

Small spring tasks. Finally, as the spring season turns over into summer, don't overlook the small maintenance jobs that make a good garden even better: Stake tall-growing plants as they grow to prevent them from falling over; tie up straying vines; and pinch new annuals to make them bushier and produce more flowers. When you thin seedlings, be ruthless. You'll have healthier plants.

Summer

Summer is the time when a well-planned and maintained garden is truly appreciated. The three big jobs—soil preparation, weeding, and watering—will all be more manageable undertakings if you have followed our suggestions for spring activities. Don't lose heart, however, if your garden work didn't go according to plan. There's still much you can do.

Weed control in flower beds or borders. By midsummer the contest between the gardener and bed or border weeds will often have been determined. If the judgment is in favor of the weeds, do something about them now before they go to seed, spreading next year's weed crop even farther. If the weeds are tall, cut them down first, using a jungle knife, rotary mower, or a nylon-string trimmer. Spread a 3-inch layer of organic soil conditioner, compost, or rotted manure over the surface and work it into the soil to a depth of 6 inches. Rake off the remaining weeds and roughly level the area. A 1-inch layer of organic mulch spread over the surface of the newly turned earth will complete your assault. If the first frosts of fall arrive later rather than earlier in your area, there is probably still time to plant any of the warm-season annuals or plan for a permanent display of perennials and shrubs.

Preparing the soil. The importance of preparing the soil as we have suggested cannot be overemphasized. Not only will all plants perform better, but weeding and watering will be kept to a minimum as well. A layer of mulch over the soil slows evaporation and keeps soil temperatures in the optimum range for plant growth. Water applied to a well-conditioned, mulched soil sinks deep into the soil, to the zone where the plants can make the best use of it, rather than staying near the surface and evaporating in the hot sun.

Watering. Lawns, vegetable gardens, trees, shrubs, and container plants all need their fair share of water during the warmer months. In areas without sufficient rains, summer watering can be among the most tedious and unrelenting of garden chores. As we have already mentioned, a layer of mulch will help plants in the open ground retain necessary moisture. But lawns, containerized gardens, and other plants have special water requirements. Automated systems—particularly sprinkler and drip systems—spell relief for the gardener. For more information on these systems, see pages 49–52. Remember the cardinal rule of waterings. When you water, water well, allowing the plants to grow strong, deep roots and remain moist. A little bit of water does more harm than good.

Pest and disease control. The summer months are also pest and disease control months. In the garden it is true that anyone looking for trouble is sure to find it, but in a sense this is good news. Problems detected in the beginning stages are invariably easier to deal with than those in full development. On your morning and evening gardening tours, make regular inspections for signs of trouble. Look for chewed or disfigured leaves, spots or moldy patches on leaves, and irregular marks on trunks and stems. Simple controls such as picking off and destroying infected leaves and stems are an important part of pest and disease control, especially in the early stages of infestation. For fruit trees and roses especially, an attentive maintenance program means that you'll ultimately have to spray less (first attacks by pests are usually the smallest and easiest to eradicate). Check at your garden center for recommendations and for information on timing.

Pruning. Summer pruning is light pruning; you can usually do it with your fingertips or with a small pair of shears. Don't underestimate finger pinching power: The growing energy in a plant constantly flows to the terminal buds, the buds at the farthest reaches of the plant. By pinching out those terminal buds, you direct the growth of the plant.

Pinching out. Many annuals need pinching out to make them bushy. Pinch out tips of sweet peas when they are 5 inches tall; pinch off the tips of snapdragons when they have only 4 or 5 leaves; marigolds and zinnias should be pinched when the first flower is formed.

For peak production of all summer flowering annuals, always pinch off faded flowers. Plants are forced to continue to produce more flowers in an effort to produce seeds. If you prevent seed production, you will be successful in keeping plants in the flowering stages. Azaleas respond very well to fingertip pruning after blooming. Simply use your thumb and finger to nip off new growth about halfway back. The plants will be bushier and produce more flowers the following season.

Fertilizing. Many plants, including most vegetables, benefit from a midseason application of fertilizer. Summer feeding is particularly necessary in areas that receive frequent summer rains, which leach nutrients from the soil. Be sure to feed shrubs that have already bloomed. A boost during this period will encourage strong, new growth well in advance of winter. The color of grass is the best indication of whether your lawn needs a summer feeding. Many will not. If the grass is a pale, yellowish green, an application of fertilizer is warranted. Otherwise, exercise caution, following fertilizer package directions for rates and timing of applications.

Fall

When it comes to garden seasons, fall is as important as spring. Spring often catches gardeners by surprise. Fall, on the other hand, usually arrives gradually and lasts long enough for gardeners to get some constructive work done.

Three important jobs are best handled in the fall: planting trees and shrubs, soil preparation, and fertilizing trees, shrubs, and lawns.

Planting trees and shrubs. In areas with all but the most severe winter climates, fall is probably the best season for planting trees and shrubs. A long fall season gives roots time to establish themselves before the really cold weather arrives. Transplant shock is reduced for trees and shrubs planted in the fall, and these plants will have a considerable headstart over the same varieties planted the following spring. Step-by-step planting instructions are given on pages 56 and 57. In severe winter climates, however, wait until spring to plant trees and shrubs.

Soil preparation and weed control. There is always an opportunity for weed work. Fall gives you another chance

Mosses and flowering bulbs give color to this spring garden.

to take action against any plot of ground where you have had a problem with weeds. Spade or rototill the soil, incorporating a 2-inch layer of organic material (such as peat moss, soil conditioner, or nitrogen stabilized sawdust) into the top 6 inches. Winter weather will have a mellowing effect on the conditioned soil, and an addition of a 1-inch layer of organic mulch after winter arrives will effectively deter sprouting weeds. Replenish the mulch in established growing areas, the rose garden, for example, with an inch or so of organic material. If you have a bed of camellias, rhododendrons, azaleas, or other acid-loving plants, use an acid-forming mulch such as pine needles, peat moss, or oak leaves.

Fertilizing. Trees, shrubs, and lawns all benefit from a fall feeding. The roots of these plants continue to grow and absorb nutrients after above-ground portions are dormant. As a rough guide for trees and shrubs, apply 1–2 pounds of fertilizer with a 10-8-7 formula for each inch of the trunk's diameter.

Lawn care. The warm-season grasses, such as Bermuda, St. Augustine, and zoysia, grow much more slowly in the fall than in spring and summer. If they are fed at this time, they will remain green longer into winter and will become green sooner in spring. If grass is thin and dominated by weeds, feeding will most likely go to the weeds. Eliminate them by hand or with a herbicide before fertilizing.

Bluegrass and other cool-season grasses will have a second growth spurt. The need to mow will be more frequent during this period, as will the need for feeding. Fertilize cool-season grass lawns twice during the fall: once in September and again in late November.

If you're not sure what kind of lawn you have, fertilize at least once in September or October with an all-purpose lawn fertilizer. Be sure you get rid of the weeds first. Fall feeding is by far the most important favor you can do for your lawn. The lawn enters winter stronger and healthier and emerges the following spring better able to resist disease and insect attacks and thick enough to deter weedy invaders.

Other miscellaneous fall jobs include:

Pruning. Winter, not fall, is the time to do major pruning, but fall *is* a good time to cut away dead limbs from trees and shrubs. With the leaves still on the plants, it is much easier to distinguish the dead and the living branches. Also remove suckers from the base of trees and shrubs.

Cleaning roses. After the final flush of roses in the fall, clean the plants by removing spent flowers and dead wood. Thoroughly rake the rose beds to help eliminate diseases and insects that may attack next year.

Composting. If you are going to use manure in the garden next spring, now is a good time to buy it. The manure should be added to a compost pile if you have one. If you don't, let the manure lie uncovered for the winter. By spring it will be well rotted and there will be no chance that it will burn tender seedlings.

Watering. Unfortunately, you can't assume that your watering responsibilities have ended just because the weather has cooled. Plants need an appropriate supply of water in fall as well as at other times, not so much for growth as to ensure winter hardiness. Be especially careful to check plants for their water needs if the season is hot or windy.

Storing garden furniture. To prevent rust and the need for another paint job, garden furniture and accessories should be pulled under cover before the first rain. If there is no storage space in the garden or shed, plastic covers designed specially for furniture are usually advertised during this time.

Winter

Winter is the time when the most pleasurable garden activity may well be daydreaming about next year's garden—the improvements you'll make and the new plants you'll try. There are chores, however.

Pruning. The most important task of winter is pruning deciduous trees and shrubs. The biggest difficulty for most people is trying to get over their fear of pruning. Heartily recommended to anyone hesitant with the shears is Ortho's *All About Pruning*. This volume carefully looks at individual plants and gives detailed instructions, in both words and illustrations, on pruning hundreds of different plants.

Spraying for insects. The second most important late winter task is spraying susceptible trees and shrubs with an oil-based dormant spray. Some of the worst summer pests—mites, whiteflies, and scale—can be destroyed with this spray, which smothers overwintering eggs and insects with the oil, rather than killing them chemically, as the spring and summer sprays do. Apply dormant oil sprays only to plants listed on the label and only on days when temperatures are above 45 degrees Fahrenheit.

Protecting plants from cold. In cold winter climates, young evergreen and other newly planted trees and shrubs should be protected from wind and severe cold. Burlap or polyethylene tacked to wooden frames, cornstalks, or straw mats are typically used to provide protection.

Feeding warm-season grasses. In warm winter areas such as south Florida, parts of the Gulf Coast, and southern California, tropical grasses—Bermuda, St. Augustine, zoysia—continue to grow throughout the winter. These grasses should be fed over the winter, following the fertilizer manufacturer's directions.

Plant Selection Guide

Browse through this list of over one hundred easy-maintenance annual and perennial flowers, shrubs, trees, and ground covers for ideas about which plants will suit your particular conditions, needs, and tastes.

The variety of easy maintenance plants is endless, and what you choose will depend on a number of factors: where you live; what you want your garden to look like, including the mix of plant types, colors, textures, and shapes; whether you want fragrant plants; and how you want to spend your maintenance time. This *Plant Selection Guide* introduces a number of plants noted for their easiness of care. Some plants, of course, require more attention than others, or more attention of certain kinds; these important aspects of maintenance are outlined in the entries.

You will read how the plants can be used, locations where they work best, and how they can make your garden a place that gives you pleasure without making you groan as you consider a long list of demands.

You will also find descriptions of the pertinent features of each plant: size, foliage color and type, flower color, and fruit. This guide can only be a first step, however. When you come upon a description of a plant that appeals to you, it is always a good idea to check with your local nursery or garden center for more details, especially to find out the particulars of cultivation for your climate and garden situation. Nursery personnel will also be familiar with a range of varieties and know which are most suitable for your area and special needs.

As you plan your garden—if you are starting from scratch—or think about how to bring the amount of time you currently spend on gardening chores more into line with the amount of time you have, first skim through this guide, making a note of those plants that appeal to you, for whatever reason: color, long-lasting periods of bloom, suitability to a special problem, or beauty in all seasons. Plants are also listed according to various categories, on pages 39 and 40. These lists will give you an overall idea of qualities to look for in selecting plants, and suggest how you might effectively blend what you like with what you need.

Zone information is based on the USDA map of climate zones, but remember that zone information is generalized; your area may be a microclimate or on a border line and not agree with the description offered. You may be successful with some plants not identified as being in your zone and not successful with plants that are. It is a good idea to double-check your plant choices with local sources of gardening information—nurseries, agricultural extensions, botanic gardens, garden clubs, universities—to make sure your plant choices will perform in your specific area and climate. Gardening neighbors and friends are also good sources of information.

Bloom dates also vary, not only among climate zones but also within your own garden, depending on such factors as weather and horticultural practices. The dates in this guide apply to USDA Climate Zone 6, a band that extends roughly horizontally from Boston through Kansas City and into the Southwest.

One of the most important tasks for an easy maintenance garden is to select plants that are well adapted, relatively pest-free, and give your garden the look you want.

Achillea millefolium
'Fire King'

Abelia × grandiflora
(Glossy Abelia)

Broad-leafed evergreen
shrub (deciduous in
the North)
Zones 6–10

Glossy abelia is the
hardiest and most
freely flowering of the
abelias. It grows at a
medium-to-fast rate,
reaching heights and
widths of 4–8 feet. Its
habit is graceful,
rounded, and arching.
Showy, pinkish white
flowers cover the plant
from July until frost;
and the finely tex-
tured, glossy, deep-
green summer foliage
turns an attractive
bronze in the fall.
Give glossy abelia
well-drained soil, half
to full sun, and aver-
age watering, and it
will grow easily, free of
pests. It can be sheared
into formal shapes, but
flowering will be re-
duced.

Acacia baileyana
(Bailey Acacia)

Evergreen tree
Zones 6–12, 14

Acacia baileyana, like
most acacias, grows
rapidly, to 20 by 20
feet, rewarding the
grower in early spring
with a mass of daffodil-
yellow flowers. The fo-
liage is blue-gray, deli-
cate, and fernlike. Cer-
tain cultivars are
available that exhibit
reddish or purple new
growth. This contrib-

Aesculus carnea 'Briottii'

Agapanthus

utes a great deal to the
year-round interest of
the plant.
A. baileyana is vir-
tually foolproof, but it
grows best in dry, well-
drained soils. Though
essentially pest-free
and maintenance-free,
the tree benefits from
some pruning when
young to assure a
pleasing branch struc-
ture.

Acanthus mollis
(Bear's Breech)

Perennial
Zones 8–10

Bear's breech is grown
for its clumps of im-
mense, coarse, dark-
green, glossy leaves

and 3-foot-tall, creamy-
white, lavender, or rose
flower spikes. It is usu-
ally considered more a
landscape plant than a
border perennial.
Bear's breech grows
best in moist, rich
loam with good drain-
age, but it performs
reasonably well in dry,
sandy soil. Though in
cool climates it can tol-
erate full sun, it pre-
fers filtered shade. It
can withstand drought,
but the foliage will be
more lush with ade-
quate moisture. In the
northern limits of its
range, plant in a
warm, protected loca-
tion, and mulch over
winter.

Alyssum saxatile

Achillea species
(Yarrow)

Perennial
All zones

Yarrow is an evergreen
herb with narrow, soft,
feathery, gray-green
leaves 1–4 inches long.
Growth habit is
spreading and rapid.
Tight clumps form a
dense, matlike cover
1–3 inches high, pro-
ducing a profusion of
clustered, tiny yellow
blossoms from spring
through summer.
Yarrow is a sturdy,
sun-loving, easy main-
tenance plant that
grows successfully in
almost any well-
drained soil and re-
quires only minimum
water during the sum-
mer. Periodic cutting of
flowers helps maintain
flower production.
Check at your local
nursery or garden cen-
ter for varieties
adapted to your area.

Aesculus parviflora
(Bottlebrush Buckeye)

Deciduous shrub
Zones 5–8

Spectacular late-
season flowers, trouble-
free foliage, and adapt-
ability to heavy shade
make the bottlebrush
buckeye an excellent
subject for a specimen
or for massing and
clumping in problem
shady areas, such as
under large shade
trees. It blooms pro-
fusely in summer, pro-
ducing white flowers
with red anthers in
large, erect clusters 8–
12 inches long.

The bottlebrush
buckeye grows easily.
It prefers moist, well-
drained soil high in or-
ganic matter, and it
tolerates full sun to
heavy shade. It is not a
shrub for small areas
because of its open,
wide-spreading (8–15
feet) suckering habit.

Agapanthus species
(Lily-of-the-Nile)

Perennial
Zones 5–10

Agapanthus is a sum-
mer-flowering peren-
nial, occurring in both
evergreen and decidu-
ous varieties. All have
leathery, straplike
leaves and fleshy roots,
varying by size and
flower color. Flowers
appear on 1–4-foot
stalks and are blue or
white, depending on
the variety.
Agapanthus is an
adaptable plant, easy
to grow in climates
with mild winters. It's
best in good garden
soil but accepts heavy
soil. Full sun allows
the fullest flowering,
though it will bloom in
some shade. Give it
ample water, particu-
larly when it is in
flower, and remove
flower stalks after
bloom. Agapanthus is
relatively pest-free.
Check at your local
nursery or garden cen-
ter for varieties
adapted to your area.
This makes an excel-
lent easy-maintenance
container plant on
decks or patios.

Arabis alpina

Arctostaphylos uva-ursi 'Radiant'

Arctotheca calendula

Armeria maritima

Ajuga species
(Bugleweed)

Perennial, used as a ground cover
Zones 5–10

The ajugas are hardy perennials, appreciated by gardeners for their ease of cultivation, fast growth, and showy flowers. The ajuga most commonly used as a ground cover is carpet bugle (*A. reptans),* which spreads by creeping stems. It is excellent for a shade ground cover (leaves become larger, more succulent) and also will accept full sun. The flowers, mostly blue, grow in spikes of 4–6 inches.

Ajugas grow best in light shade. Good garden soil with fast drainage is necessary, or nematodes and fungus diseases are likely to appear. Water moderately, every 7–10 days in summer, more

in full sun. Do not allow plants to dry out. In cold-winter areas, protect from winter winds with organic mulch. To rejuvenate plants, mow lightly after blooming. Check at your local nursery or garden center for varieties adapted to your area.

Alyssum saxatile
(Basket-of-Gold, Gold-Dust, Madwort)

Perennial
Zones 3–10

Basket-of-gold is a hardy perennial and classic rock garden plant best known for its bright, golden-yellow flower clusters in spring. It grows to about 12 inches high, and the grayish green leaves are 2–5 inches long.

Basket-of-gold likes full sun and a warm spot in the garden. It will accept most well-drained soils (on the

dry side), but if the soil is very rich growth is coarser. Stimulate compact growth by cutting back stems after flowering.

Arabis species
(Rock Cress)

Ground cover
Zones 6–10

The rock cresses are typically border and rock garden plants, not large-scale ground covers but perfect as "nook and cranny" plants. They are easily grown, producing fragrant white, pink, or rosy purple flowers in spring or early summer.

Rock cress needs heat and full sun. Once established, the plants require little water and are essentially drought-tolerant. After flowering, cut back the upright stems to induce more horizontal growth. One plant will cover a square foot.

Arctostaphylos uva-ursi
(Bearberry, Manzanita, Kinnikinick)

Broad-leafed evergreen
Zones 2–8A

A low, mat-forming ground cover with evergreen foliage of pleasing, fine texture, bearberry is especially useful for poor, sandy soil. Drooping, tiny, bell-shaped flowers— not particularly showy, but attractive—are followed by bright red berries.

Bearberry will give complete cover in about two seasons if plants are set from containers or flats 2 feet apart. It is salt-tolerant and makes an excellent beach plant.

Arctotheca calendula
(Cape Gold)

Tender perennial
Zone 10

Cape gold is a long-blooming, fast-growing perennial that provides color most of the year. Gray-green leaves form a fairly dense cover 3–10 inches high studded with yellow, daisylike flowers about 2 inches in diameter.

Cape gold grows well in any soil with good drainage, but it needs full sun and regular watering. The plant, though tender to frost, can recover from short

exposure to 32 degrees Fahrenheit. It is easier to maintain than a grass lawn, requiring high mowing (4–5 inches) only every year or so.

Armeria species
(Thrift, Sea Pink)

Perennial, used as a ground cover
All zones

Common thrift is a sturdy, evergreen perennial that grows in dense, grassy clumps, producing an abundance of tightly clustered, delicate, pink or white flowers, three-fourths inch across, at the ends of long, thin stems. Height can range from 2-inch tufts and 3–5-inch stems, to 10-inch tufts with flowers rising above 2 feet. Growth rate is slow. Thrift blooms continuously in the spring, into summer in inland areas, even longer in coastal and cooler areas. Clumps spread to about 15 inches.

Thrift will grow in almost any soil but needs good drainage and full sun to thrive. It requires only moderate watering during hot summer months. To ensure accurate reproduction, propagate plants by division. Check at your local nursery or garden center for varieties adapted to your area.

Aronia arbutifolia

Asclepias tuberosa

Aucuba japonica

Aronia arbutifolia
(Red Chokeberry)

Deciduous shrub
Zones 5–8B

The red chokeberry is a distinctly leggy, upright, slow-growing shrub that reaches heights of 6–10 feet and widths of 3–5 feet. It produces bright-red berries and showy fall color ranging from red to purple. Planting in masses accentuates the fruit display and diminishes its legginess.

Able to tolerate dry soils and prairie drought, red chokeberry is also an excellent choice for problem wet areas. Fruiting is best in full sun, although partial shade is tolerated well. Adaptable to any soil (even heavy clay) and little troubled by pests, the red chokeberry is a care-free plant.

Asclepias tuberosa
(Butterfly Flower, Butterfly Weed)

Perennial
Zones 3–10

Plants, which grow from 18 to 36 inches high, are composed of clusters of erect stems branched toward the top, giving them an erect and slightly spreading form. Their leaves are dark green and hairy. Brilliant orange-red clusters of flowers appear in summer to attract hordes of butterflies, hummingbirds, and bees to the garden.

Native to meadows and prairies, asclepias is best in light, sandy, poor soil and full sun and will tolerate wind. Expect good performance in peaty soil or even heavy clay. Avoid excessively moist soils. Water only through drought, especially in heavy soils. There are no serious pests.

Athyrium species
(Lady Fern, Japanese Painted Fern)

Perennial, used as a ground cover
All zones

Athyriums are deciduous, delicate, 2–4-foot ferns, unusually easy to grow. The most common variety is the lady fern *(Athyrium filix-femina)*, with a vase-like shape and yellow-green fronds. This variety tolerates more sun and less moisture than most ferns and spreads thickly enough to compete successfully against most weeds. The Japanese painted fern, *A. goeringianum,* grows to 1½ feet and has slightly drooping fronds, remarkable for their coloring. Stems and main veins are ruby red and fronds are a soft gray-green, creating contrast.

Athyriums will grow just about anywhere. Protection from wind will keep the fronds from becoming ragged. Ideal conditions include a well-prepared soil kept moist, with some shade. Check at your local nursery or garden center for species adapted to your area.

Aucuba japonica
(Japanese Aucuba)

Broad-leafed evergreen shrub
Zones 7B–10

The Japanese aucuba is valued for its tolerance of heavy shade; its leathery, large, evergreen leaves; and its adaptability to adverse growing conditions. Unpruned, the shrub becomes a leggy, open plant that grows 6–10 feet or taller. Pruning will keep it dense and round. Use Japanese aucuba in that problem shady area, such as a dim, north-facing entryway or under densely foliaged trees. It also makes an excellent container plant.

Performing well in any soil and drought-tolerant once established, Japanese aucuba still benefits from additional organic matter in the soil when it is planted. It is not a plant for hot, sunny, exposed locations.

Berberis thunbergii
(Japanese Barberry)

Deciduous shrub
Zones 5–9

The Japanese barberry is a popular hedge and barrier plant. It is extremely easy to grow, with impenetrable, thorny stems and dense, finely textured, shearable foliage. Growing at a moderate rate, 3–6 feet high and 4–7 feet wide, its natural outline is upright, arching, and rounded.

This barberry is extremely adaptable to nearly any soil, withstands drought well, and performs admirably in full sun or partial shade. It can be easily transplanted.

Calendula officinalis
(Pot Marigold)

Annual
All zones

The pot marigold is known for broad expanses of color over a very long season. Two successive plantings, one in spring and one in summer, will give color well into fall. In mild climates, the pot marigold blooms well all winter long. It is hardy enough to withstand temperatures several degrees below freezing. The large, 3–5-inch blossoms can be daisylike and single or double like chrysanthemums. The flowers are borne on strong stems ideal for cutting, especially the taller, 2-foot varieties. Foliage is a clean, attractive dark green.

The pot marigold is not fussy. It performs well in containers and is accepting of a wide range of cultural conditions. It self-sows readily and in mild climates will naturalize beautifully in the "wild" garden.

Callistemon citrinus
(Lemon Bottlebrush)

Broad-leafed evergreen shrub
Zones 9 and 10

Common in the gardens of southern California and Florida, this evergreen plant displays throughout the year striking, bright-red, brushlike flowers that are attractive to hummingbirds. Its fragrant leaves are lemon scented. A massive shrub, growing 10–15 feet in height and width into a round-headed open form, the lemon bottlebrush is

Calycanthus floridus

Berberis thunbergii atropurpurea

best used as a screen, a tall, informal hedge, or possibly as a specimen.

Lemon bottlebrush is an excellent choice for the desert landscape, since it tolerates drought and a wide range of soils from alkaline to saline. Good drainage and full sun are preferred.

Calycanthus floridus
(Carolina Allspice, Strawberry Shrub)

Deciduous shrub
Zones 5–9

For fragrance in bloom and easy care, the Carolina allspice is hard to beat. The 2-inch, dull, reddish brown flowers, while merely "interesting" to look at, permeate the garden with a sweet strawberry scent in May and, often, sporadically into July. The shrub grows slowly to a neat, rounded outline, 6–9 feet high and 6–12 feet wide.

Carolina allspice will grow in nearly any soil but performs best in deep, moist loam. While adaptable to both sun and shade, it will not grow as tall in full sun. The shrub transplants readily and is highly resistant to pests. Prune after flowering.

Calendula officinalis

Caragana arborescens
(Siberian Pea Shrub)

Deciduous shrub
Zones 2–7

Valuable for use as a hedge, screen, or windbreak where growing conditions are difficult—especially in the northern plains states—the Siberian pea shrub contributes bright-yellow flowers to the May landscape. A large shrub, growing rapidly into a 15-foot-high and 12-foot-wide, sparse, angular, and open structure, it is often trained as a small tree.

The Siberian pea shrub grows well in dry, rocky soils and exposed, windy sites, a

good plant to know about for difficult spots. It resists most pests, although it can be susceptible to leafhoppers.

Carpinus betulus
(European hornbeam)

Deciduous tree
Zones 2–8

The European hornbeam is a neat, manageable, attractive tree with dark green, elm-like foliage turning to yellow in the fall; smooth gray bark; and interesting nutlike fruit clusters. It retains its dark leaves until spring. One of the best trees for hedges and screens, and also an excellent street tree, it is sold in

the trade as 'Fastigiata' and 'Pyramidalis'. 'Columnaris' is similar, but it spreads more. *Carpinus caroliniana*, an American native, has many of the good qualities of the European hornbeam, but it is slightly hardier and has more intense yellow or reddish fall color.

The European hornbeam stands soils from dry and rocky to wet but well-drained, and is tolerant of air pollution.

Celtis species
(Hackberry)

Deciduous tree
Zones 6 and 7

Three hackberries are common to the western states: *Celtis occiden-*

Caragana arborescens

talis, C. australis, and *C. sinensis.* All are wonderful trees for tough, arid regions. The common hackberry, *C. occidentalis,* is the most widely available, but it is less desirable than the other two because of its irregular, spreading growth; *C. sinensis* is less widely available. *C. australis* has dark-green leaves with finely toothed edges and bears small, edible, dark-purple berries prized by birds.

Use *C. australis* as a shade or lawn tree or even as a street tree. It is drought-tolerant and can stand hot, dry winds and city conditions. Pests are not particularly a problem.

Cercidiphyllum japonicum

Convallaria majalis

Cistus hybrid

Cercidiphyllum japonicum
(Katsura Tree)

Deciduous tree
Zones 3 and 4

The katsura tree, when trained as a single-trunked tree, is upright and narrow, but spreading and vase-shaped with age. Left multitrunked, it is broad and spreading, branching upward and outward, eventually reaching heights to 40 feet or more. Leaves are a lustrous reddish to reddish purple in spring when they first unfold. In the summer, foliage is dark green, neat, and crisp, turning scarlet and gold in the fall. Small dry fruit capsules provide winter ornamentation.

This is an excellent tree for providing filtered shade. It is pest-free and tolerant of moist soil and shade.

Chaenomeles speciosa
(Common Flowering Quince)

Deciduous shrub
Zones 5–9

The common flowering quince is the most ornamental of the quinces. It is a single-season plant that produces showy flowers lasting about 10 days in spring. Quince can remain in bloom for a much longer period of time. Variable in habit, it is usually a rounded, dense shrub 6–10 feet high and as wide, with thorns. Cultivars are available from prostrate to open to erect forms, some of which are thornless.

Common flowering quince is easy to grow and adaptable to a wide variety of conditions and soils, including dry soils and prairie drought. This quince flowers most prolifically when it is placed in full sun and when it is pruned annually to about 6 inches from the ground immediately after spring bloom. It can be pruned anytime, however, to create a special effect, such as an oriental look. Place quince where the surrounding soil does not need to be cultivated regularly. Otherwise, suckering can become a problem.

Cistus species
(Rock Rose)

Broad-leafed evergreen
Zones 8–10

Useful in the Mediterranean-type climates of the West, the rock roses make an excellent large-scale bank and ground cover that can be effective in controlling erosion. They are easy to maintain and big in spring color. The foliage is fragrant, especially on hot days. Drought-resistant and adaptable to salt spray, ocean winds, and desert heat, rock roses are bushy, dense, rounded shrubs that generally grow 3–4 feet tall and 4–5 feet wide. When massed they give the effect of a billowing dark or gray green sea of foliage.

Give rock roses fast-draining soil, and pinch the tips of young plants to encourage denser growth. Do not plan to move them once they're established because they don't transplant well. Check your local nursery or garden center for varieties adapted to your area.

Clethra alnifolia
(Summersweet, Sweet Pepperbush)

Deciduous shrub
Zones 3–9

Summersweet blooms in July and August, when flowers are scarce, producing extremely fragrant, cool-white spikes. Once established, it grows slowly to a broad, oval mass 3–8 feet high and 4–8 feet wide that rarely needs pruning. It is cloaked in handsome, dark-green, pest-free foliage that inconsistently turns a clear yellow in the fall before dropping.

Summersweet is especially useful in wet, shady areas of the garden; and it is quite tolerant of salty, sandy coastal conditions. But its best garden performance is in moist, acid soil that is heavily supplemented with organic matter. The soil should be well drained.

This plant is particularly well adapted to the Middle Atlantic states and to parts of the Pacific Northwest.

Convallaria majalis
(Lily-of-the-Valley)

Bulb, used as a ground cover
Zones 2–7

Lily-of-the-valley is a very hardy and adaptable ground cover. It thrives in partial or full shade and develops a dense mass of soil-holding roots. Leaves die back in the fall and are renewed in spring. New leaves grow to 8 inches long and 1–3 inches wide. The fragrant, quarter-inch, usually white, bell-shaped flowers appear in spring. These are fully hardy plants but do not thrive in mild-climate areas.

Lily-of-the-valley is an undemanding plant that grows in just about any soil, but it prefers rich soil with ample organic matter and periodic feeding. Planted on 7-inch centers, plants spread into a ground cover that needs little attention. Watering requirements are average.

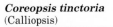
Coreopsis 'Goldfink'

Cotoneaster microphyllus 'Cochleatus'

Elaeagnus pungens 'Maculata'

Coreopsis tinctoria
(Calliopsis)

Annual
All zones

Coreopsis is a work-horse in borders or in beds; it blooms from late spring to early fall. If the longest possible blooming is desired, remove spent blossoms at least once a week. Flowers are yellow to red, bronze, and pink. Coreopsis is at its best when naturalized in dry meadows or in "rough" zones between lawns and wild places. It will thrive if left alone, providing continual color. Coreopsis will show considerable variation when naturalized, including the dwarf varieties.

Plant in full sun and dryish soil. Coreopsis is drought-tolerant.

Cotoneaster species
(Cotoneaster)

Shrub, used as a ground cover
All zones

Many cotoneasters are suitable as ground covers. Among them are varieties adapted to virtually every climate of North America. They are deep-rooted and will control erosion, each variety producing attractive flowers in spring and berries in fall.

Cotoneasters are tough and hardy, pest-free plants requiring little maintenance. They're easy to grow and transplant, thriving in heavy clay soil. Full sun is best. Occasionally, dead or awkward branches need to be removed. Otherwise prune only to encourage the graceful arching of the branches. Since some cotoneasters respond poorly to pruning, often producing ugly, twiggy growth, plant far enough from paths and patios so they do not interfere with traffic. Check at your local nursery or garden center for varieties adapted to your area.

Crataegus species
(Hawthorn)

Deciduous tree
Zones 1–8, 16

The hawthorns, among the toughest of flowering trees, are all quite similar, thorny, small trees. With few exceptions, they bear white flowers (blooming after most of the spring-flowering trees have finished) and have showy red or orange fruits. Many species have fine glossy foliage, and the fruits of most are exceptionally long lasting. Their picturesque and wide-spreading habit make

Crataegus laevigata 'Rosea'

them a landscape asset even in the midst of winter.

Hawthorns thrive even in adverse situations—in the inner city, along highways, and at the seashore, where salt spray is a hazard to most trees. They are particularly useful for making trespasser-proof hedges because of their sharp thorns.

Prune as necessary to thin or to control fire-blight, and watch for aphids.

Deutzia gracilis
(Slender Deutzia)

Deciduous shrub
Zones 5–8

Of the many deutzia species and cultivars, slender deutzia is probably the most graceful in form and the most

dependable for flower. A low, broad-mounded shrub 2–6 feet high and 3–6 feet wide with gracefully upright, arching branches and dull-green foliage, this shrub is best used in a shrub border, where its nondescript appearance when not in flower can blend with other shrubs. In May, pure white flowers literally cover the shrub like a bank of new snow.

Slender deutzia is easy to grow and transplants readily in the spring into any reasonably good garden soil. Give it full sun to light shade.

Elaeagnus angustifolia
(Russian Olive, Silverberry)

Deciduous tree
Zones 2–8

The Russian olive is a small tree, growing quickly to 20–25 feet high and wide. Its leaves are willowlike, olive-green above, silvery beneath. The dark-brown bark is attractive on the usually crooked, twisted trunk. Branches are thorny. Greenish yellow, fragrant flowers in early summer are followed by quantities of yellow berries that furnish winter food for many birds. Use this tree

with great effect as a hedge, screen, or wind-break and as a means for erosion control.

The Russian olive is a tough tree, widely adaptable to all but poorly drained soils. It does well in hot, dry areas, but it does not like cool, moist coastal conditions. Watering requirements are minimal to average.

Elaeagnus pungens
(Silverberry)

Broad-leafed evergreen shrub
Zones 7–10

The silverberry is a tough, adaptable shrub with inconspicuous but powerfully fragrant flowers that bloom in fall, and evergreen, olive-colored foliage, thorny branches, and edible red fruit in the spring. It is an excellent hedge plant, its thorny branches presenting an impenetrable barrier. Without pruning it rapidly becomes a rigid, sprawling, angular shrub growing anywhere from 6 to 15 feet tall.

Good in problem areas of heat, wind, and drought, this shrub actually prefers poor, infertile soil, because it fixes its own nitrogen from the atmosphere. It responds well to shearing, which increases its density.

Eschscholzia californica

Euonymus alata

Eucalyptus citriodora

Eschscholzia californica
(California Poppy)

Annual
All zones

In springs after winters with heavy rainfall, the California poppy, the state flower of California, literally covers the rolling grasslands and semi-desert plains in cheerful, golden orange. Hybrids present an expanded range of color and blossom types. Foliage is feathery bluish green.

Sow seeds in the fall if you have mild, wet winters; in the early spring otherwise, giving plenty of water either way to break seed dormancy. California poppy prefers sandy, alkaline soil with excellent drainage. Full sun is best, but partial shade is acceptable. It tolerates drought and poor, dry soils. It performs beautifully in dry, well-drained borders and beds, and is best in informal settings where its reseeding tendency can be tolerated. Successful transplanting is difficult.

Eucalyptus species
(Eucalyptus)

Broad-leafed evergreen tree
Zones 8–10

Eucalyptus are essentially foolproof and maintenance-free. Nothing quite compares with their form—tall, graceful, evergreen, and responsive to the slightest breeze. Flowers vary in size, color, and type; leaves of almost all types have a characteristic pungency. This family has a vitality totally lacking in most other trees of comparable stature. Perhaps a half dozen of the many species are suitable for the home garden.

Eucalyptus grow rapidly, so they should be set out at the smallest practical size and given as little support as possible. Trees grow broader than tall for the first six months, and the resulting tapered trunk is able to withstand strong winds. Most species are drought-tolerant and pest-free. Check your local nursery or garden center for varieties adapted to your area.

Euonymus alata
(Burning Bush, Winged Euonymus)

Deciduous shrub
Zones 4–7

Euonymus alata is popular for its brilliant-scarlet fall color, its neat, vase-shaped habit, and its clean, pest-free foliage. Mature shrubs are quite large and open, however—15–20 feet high and as wide. Flowers are small; fruit is bright orange-red. Use it as an unclipped hedge or screen, in groups, in the shrub border, or as a specimen.

Burning bush is easily transplanted and adaptable to many soils and growing conditions, except to very wet ones. It adapts equally well to full sun or heavy shade, where it still develops good fall color, although its brightest hues are in full sun. Pruning destroys the neat outline of the plant. Water moderately.

Euonymus fortunei
(Wintercreeper)

Evergreen vine or shrub
Zones 5–10

Wintercreeper functions well as a ground cover when it is allowed to grow flat, with nothing to climb. Pointed, somewhat leathery, dark-green, jagged leaves, 1½–2 inches long, are set oppositely along trailing stems, which often root where they touch moist soil. Flowers, only occasionally produced, are inconspicuous. Its habit varies, depending on how it is used and the cultivar chosen.

Wintercreepers are hardy, sturdy plants that will grow in most parts of the country, in sun or shade, good or poor soil. They are drought-resistant but do not do well in hot desert areas even when adequately watered.

Fothergilla major
(Large Fothergilla)

Deciduous shrub
Zones 6–8

Fothergilla is one of the most attractive and desirable of the southeastern native shrubs. Its honey-scented, profuse white blooms, appearing in late April–May, resemble small, round bottlebrushes. Its clean, dark-green,

Gaillardia pulchella

and pest-free foliage consistently provides an extremely showy fall display of electric yellow, orange, and scarlet. It is an exceptionally neat, rounded shrub that grows 6–10 feet high with a slightly narrower spread. Use fothergilla in groups, masses, and foundation planting. It is especially attractive as a specimen or integrated into a shrub border.

Although an acid, well-drained soil is a must, fothergilla is a relatively adaptable plant that is entirely pest-free. It grows well in partial shade and dry, rocky soils, but full sun and soils rich in organic matter improve flowers and fall color. Watering requirements are average.

Genista

Gleditsia triacanthos inermis 'Sunburst'

Gazania splendens

Gaillardia pulchella
(Blanket Flower)

Annual
All zones

Gaillardia pulchella sports yellow, red, or bicolored flowers on leafless stems above deep-green leaves. It blooms from June to frost. Gaillardias are a little rough and loose for a formal bed or border, but they are excellent to mix with other plants in rustic and natural settings. Place them in small groups at the edge of a lawn or scatter them in a meadow.

Plant gaillardias in open, breezy spaces and light, sandy soil on the alkaline side. Allow for full sun. Too much moisture, either in heavy soil or standing on the leaves, will cause problems.

Gazania species
(Gazania)

Tender perennial, used as a ground cover
Zones 9 and 10

There are many species and hybrids, but the only significant differences among them are growth habit and color. Trailing gazania (*Gazania rigens leucolaena*) and its hybrids have a trailing habit, spreading rapidly by fast-rooting runners. The others grow in clumps. Trailing types

are better for covering slopes. Gazania flowers span the color spectrum. All bloom from late spring through summer and intermittently the rest of the time. Like osteospermum and some other plants with daisylike flowers, they close up at night and on dark days. Foliage is typically grayish, fairly dense, and reaches a height of 2½–6 inches. Flowers are 1½–3 inches across; some of the hybrids are larger (3–4 inches), appearing at the top of 3–10-inch upright stems.

Gazanias grow satisfactorily in moist soils having good drainage. They must have a warm, sunny location and two or three waterings a month in hot weather. Gazanias are subject to fungus diseases that cause dieback and require replanting of damaged areas. They are frost-tender but will stand cold better than arctotheca. Check with your local nursery or garden center for varieties adapted to your area.

Genista tinctoria
(Common Woadwaxen)

Deciduous shrub
Zones 2–9

Genista tinctoria, the hardiest of the brooms, features spectacular yellow flowers in June

and a small, neat, rounded habit that is 2–3 feet high, composed of strongly vertical, nearly leafless, evergreen stems.

All genistas require full sun and good drainage, but beyond that they are easy to grow and adaptable, actually preferring poor, dry, infertile soil. They tolerate drought and coastal conditions well. Leave genistas where planted after they become established—they do not move easily.

Ginkgo biloba
(Maidenhair Tree)

Deciduous tree
Zones 2–12

The maidenhair tree's picturesque, irregular habit of growth is most interesting, as are the bright-green, fan-shaped leaves. They turn brilliant yellow in fall and drop all at once—sometimes overnight—a plus for those who like to rake only once. The tree's growth rate varies with climate, and it can reach heights of 60–100 feet. Usually it is somewhat conical and sparsely branched in youth, becoming more spreading and denser with age. The maidenhair is an excellent park or large lawn tree, needing room to develop.

The maidenhair tree

is a remarkably tough tree that stands smoke and air pollution and ranks as one of the top ten trees for wide streets. It is pest-free and widely adaptable, demanding only a well-drained soil. Water in dry seasons until the tree reaches 10–20 feet; then leave it on its own.

Gleditsia species
(Honey Locust)

Deciduous tree
Zones 5–9

The honey locust is an excellent fast-growing lawn and street tree. It reaches heights of 35–70 feet, with a straight and thorny trunk and arching branches. Leaves are delicate and compound, with tiny leaflets, allowing filtered sunlight through. The lacy appearance gives the tree

an almost tropical look. Honey locusts favor good lawn growth because of their light shade and their leafing cycle. Leafing out occurs late in the spring, and leaves are dropped early in the fall, thus giving turf extra sun.

Honey locust has performed especially well in difficult, inner-city plantings. It tolerates well various environmental stresses, including air pollution and highway salting. Raking chores are minimal because the leaves are small and blend into grass. In certain southern localities the honey locust can be troubled by mimosa webworm, pod gall, and plant bugs. Check your local nursery or garden center for varieties adapted to your area.

Hamamelis × intermedia 'Ruby Glow'

Hedera helix

Hemerocallis 'May Hall'

Hamamelis × intermedia
(Hybrid Witch Hazel)

Deciduous shrub
Zones 6–8

All witch hazels are delightful for their spicily fragrant, delicately showy winter flowers. Although *Hamamelis × intermedia* is not as fragrant or restrained in size as others, it is the showiest of all the witch hazels available in the United States. As early as February its leafless branches can be covered with deep-yellow blossoms that last about a month. This is not a shrub for small gardens—it will eventually reach 15–20 feet in height with a comparable spread. Expect an outstanding show of fall color in reds, oranges, and yellows before the leaves drop.

Hamamelis × intermedia is an easy-to-grow, dramatic plant for large gardens and open spaces.

Hedera species
(Ivy)

Vine, used as a ground cover
Zones 6–9

As a ground cover, ivy does almost everything: stays green the entire year, spreads rapidly, lies flat, climbs and covers, prevents erosion, provides insulation, works in sun or shade, adapts to most climates, requires minimal care, and is easily propagated. Besides all that, it can be enormously attractive. Generally, self-branching and compact growers give the densest cover.

An ivy bed is most easily begun with well-established plants, which can be purchased in pots or flats. Ivy requires a well-draining soil. It grows best in indirect light, but once established will tolerate full sun or even fairly heavy, though not deep, shade. Maintenance of the ivy bed is easy. Mow it every other year (just prior to new growth) with the mower at the highest setting to keep the growth from becoming dense enough to harbor undesirable animal life. The plants will be covered with leaves with the first growth of spring. Check your local nursery or garden center for varieties adapted to your area.

Hemerocallis species
(Daylily)

Perennial, sometimes used as a tall ground cover
Zones 3–10

Daylilies are long-lasting perennials with attractive foliage and showy flowers. The individual blossoms last only a day but are continuously produced over a long season. Blooms come in many colors—shades of cream, yellow, orange, red, pink, and violet—often striped and bicolored. Individually they are from 3 to 5 inches long, and open just as wide. Plants, including flowers, may grow to 4 feet tall. Some varieties are very fragrant. Daylilies are exceedingly long-lived, and clumps will expand indefinitely. They are restrained in growth, permanent, not invasive, and compete well with roots of trees and shrubs.

Daylilies are easy to grow. They are highly adaptable but perform best in well-drained soil high in organic matter and of only average fertility. Tolerating shade or sun well, they seem to prefer full sun in northern areas and partial shade in the hot South. Water through dry periods and feed lightly occasionally. Most varieties can be left alone permanently, but some of the more vigorous ones give improved performance with division every six or seven years. The plant has no serious pests.

Hosta species
(Plantain Lily, Funkia)

Perennial
Zones 3–10

The plantain lilies are a large and valuable group of deciduous perennials valued mainly for their dramatic heart-shaped, glossy leaves. They're hardy, long-lived, and one of the best plants to grow in shade. All varieties are deciduous—they die to the ground each winter and are renewed each spring. Plantain lilies are excellent border plants and have long been used to edge perennial beds or shrubs. Where shade is too heavy, as it can be under trees or facing a northern exposure, plantain lilies are of great practical value. Planted singly as accent plants, they can be used to break up the monotony of many smaller-leafed plants.

Hostas are easy to grow. They need regular summer watering and prefer a sandy or

Hosta 'Thomas Hogg'

Ilex cornuta 'Rotunda'

Ilex vomitoria 'Nana'

loamy soil, high in organic matter, that has good drainage. Medium-to-dense shade is a necessity. To propagate them, dig and divide when growth first begins in spring. Bait for snails and slugs—they love the leaves—three or four times a year.

Hypericum prolificum
(Shrubby St. Johnswort)

Deciduous shrub
Zones 5–9

Shrubby St. Johnswort is the hardiest hypericum, a dense, rounded shrub that grows 1–4 feet high and wide. Its bright-yellow flowers have a long season, spanning most of the summer. The foliage is blue-green and clean. Use shrubby St. Johnswort in a border, for large-scale masses or small groupings, as foundation plantings, or as a low, informal hedge.

Hypericum is a tough, durable plant that's easy to maintain and free from pests. Plant in a location with bright sun and well-drained, light soil. It tolerates poor, dry, sterile soil, city air pollution, and partial shade beautifully. Although seldom necessary, pruning should be done in the late spring after new growth hardens off.

Ilex cornuta
(Chinese Holly)

Broad-leafed evergreen
Zones 7–10

While the species is a large, upright shrub 10–15 feet tall, many smaller, denser cultivars of this shrub are available. The leaves are an extremely handsome, dark, polished green in all seasons, larger and coarser than the Japanese holly. The fruits are normally a brilliant red and bear profusely. Unlike other hollies, the fruits apparently develop without fertilization, so having both male and female plants is not necessary.

Chinese holly does well in sun or shade and is tolerant of pollution. It is easily transplanted and thrives best in moist, well-drained, slightly acid soil. Pruning should be done after new growth matures in the spring.

Ilex crenata
(Japanese Holly)

Broad-leafed evergreen
Zones 6B–10

This holly is commonly mistaken for boxwood due to its neat, rounded shape and dark-green, dense, lustrous, and finely textured foliage. A slow-growing shrub that responds well to pruning, it will eventually reach 5–10 feet in height with a usually greater spread, although old specimens in arboreta often reach 20 feet or more. A wide range of cultivars is available for size, form, and hardiness. The Japanese holly makes an excellent selection for hedges, foundation planting, and massing, and for an evergreen, soft texture in a shrub border.

Japanese holly transplants easily into moist, well-drained, slightly acid soils, does well in sun or shade, and appears to be tolerant of pollution. Often sheared into formal shapes, the plants should be pruned after the new growth has matured in the spring. Unlike some hollies, the fruits are black and inconspicuous.

Ilex vomitoria
(Yaupon)

Broad-leafed evergreen
Zones 7B–10

While the species is a small evergreen tree, several cultivars are available, such as 'Nana' and 'Stokes', that are effectively dwarf (18 inches or less) and compact. Yaupon's finely textured foliage can easily be sheared into formal shapes, and while the species is considered one of the heaviest fruiting of the hollies, the dwarf forms are generally sterile.

Yaupon, a popular plant in the southeastern United States, is more tolerant of alkaline soils and drought than other hollies.

Juniperus species
(Juniper)

Coniferous shrub, sometimes used as a ground cover
Zones 2–10

The juniper is extremely versatile and adaptable to nearly any growing condition; it is also one of the original easy maintenance plants. Juniper types include ground covers and shrubs growing to almost any height, width, and shape. The foliage is needlelike, scalelike, or both.

When well located and established, there is a juniper to solve nearly any landscape problem. While preferring sandy, well-drained soil and a sunny, open exposure, they will grow well just about anywhere, in any soil, provided it isn't water-logged or in deep shade. Guard against overwatering junipers or planting them in the path of lawn-oriented sprinkler systems. When you plant, be sure to account for mature size. Although easy to grow, junipers have varying susceptibility to a range of pests, including twig blight, bagworms, white juniper scale, spider mites, spruce mites, twig borers, root rot, and water molds. When planted in shade they quickly become spindly and loose. In wet soils they are especially susceptible to disease. Check your local nursery or garden center for varieties adapted to your area.

Kerria japonica

Kniphofia uvaria

Kerria japonica
(Japanese Kerria)

Deciduous shrub
Zones 5–9

Japanese kerria has bright-yellow flowers in the spring and bright-green stems all winter long. Use it in a border and in masses and groups where shade is a problem. It grows moderately to 9 feet and can get an equal spread.

A tough, care-free shrub, Japanese kerria should be planted in a protected location with good drainage to reduce the chance of winter damage. Avoid rich, fertile soils, which cause the plant to become rank and weedy and decrease flower production. Water until the plant is established; then leave it alone. Prune directly after flowering since it flowers on last year's wood.

Kniphofia uvaria
(Torch Lily, Red-Hot Poker)

Perennial
Zones 7–10

The torch lily produces gracefully arching mounds of grasslike leaves and rigid, erect spikes of brilliant flowers that create an exotic, almost tropical effect. The flowers are flaming red or red-orange, blending into

yellow below. The species blooms in August and September, the hybrids in June, July, or August.

For best cultivation of *Kniphofia uvaria,* the soil must be well drained; soggy conditions are usually deadly. Avoid windy spots, as taller spikes may get damaged or broken, and they are difficult to stake attractively. Give the plant full sun only. Mulch over winter where temperatures drop to 0 degrees Fahrenheit and below. There are no serious pests. Division may be needed every fourth or fifth year, but most clumps can go indefinitely without disturbance. Divide in early spring to increase your supply of this plant.

Koelreuteria paniculata
(Golden-Rain Tree, Varnish Tree)

Deciduous tree
Zones 1–10

The golden-rain tree grows quickly while young and by the age of 15 or 20 years displays a mature, well-proportioned form (20–35 feet high by 10–40 feet wide) that requires little or no pruning to maintain a pleasant symmetry. It leafs out in April, in soft, medium-green, divided

leaves, followed in late spring by masses of yellow flowers, attractive to bees. Fruits are produced if the tree is regularly watered. Its open, branching habit giving slight shade allows grass to grow beneath the branches.

The golden-rain tree is well adapted to harsh climates; it tolerates high winds, alkaline soil, long periods without much water (except when young), and low winter temperatures.

Kolkwitzia amabilis
(Beautybush)

Deciduous shrub
Zones 5–8

Beautybush is spectacular when it is in bloom. The bright-pink flowers are produced in late spring in great profusion. Beautybush is a large shrub with medium texture in the summer and coarse texture in the winter. It grows rapidly to 6–10 feet high (sometimes 12 feet) and has a slightly smaller spread. The upright-arching form usually becomes quite leggy, but the reddish, peeling bark of the lower trunks and branches can be quite attractive.

Beautybush is an easy maintenance shrub, easily transplanted, and indifferent to soil type. Give it

Lagerstroemia indica

a sunny location and plenty of room to grow, and prune out older stems every year. Old, overgrown shrubs can be renewed by cutting them to the ground. Prune after flowering, since it blooms on old wood. Water needs are average.

Lagerstroemia indica
(Crepemyrtle, Crape Myrtle)

Deciduous shrub
Zones 7B–10

Actually a small tree, most forms of crepemyrtle can be grown as large, upright-rounded shrubs, 15–25 feet high and as wide. Several dwarf cultivars 5–12 feet tall are also available. New foliage is bronze, maturing to

a medium green, then turning into electric reds, yellows, or oranges in the fall. Flowers are produced from mid to late summer in great profusion, ranging in shade from purple to red to white. Crepemyrtle flowers on the current season's growth, so it can be pruned as late as early spring and still produce flowers the same season.

Plant crepemyrtle in well-drained, moist soil rich in organic matter and in a hot, sunny location. Spray to control aphids. If possible, plant dwarf cultivars that will be resistant to powdery mildew. Otherwise, you will need to spray just before blooming every year.

Lantana camara hybrid

Laurus nobilis

Lavandula angustifolia

**Leptospermum
scoparium**

Lantana camara
(Trailing Lantana)

Tender perennial, used
as a ground cover
Zones 9 and 10

Trailing lantana (*Lantana montevidensis,*
sometimes called *L.
sellowiana*) is a perennial evergreen shrub
in areas where temperatures do not fall much
below freezing. Its popularity is due to its
general toughness,
rapid growth, and recurring, year-long display of lavender
flowers. Small clusters
of tiny flowers appear
along the ends of vinelike stems lined with
oval, dark-green
leaves. The stems, 3–4
feet long, root as they
spread. A planting will

reach a height of 1½–2
feet. A number of varieties are available in
different colors. Trailing lantana is good for
large-scale planting,
particularly on steep
banks where maintenance is a problem. It
is perhaps too coarse
textured for covering
larger areas around
the home, but it is very
useful for borders or
edging.

Trailing lantana
needs only sun to
thrive. It grows well in
poor soil and is
drought-resistant,
needing only occasional watering. Old
stands get woody and
develop dead patches
that should be cut in
early spring.

Laurus nobilis
(Sweet Bay, Grecian
Laurel)

Evergreen tree
Zones 6–10

Sweet bay is a well-
behaved, slow-growing,
indoor-outdoor tree
reaching heights of
12–40 feet. It has a
very sophisticated look
and takes well to
shearing into hedges,
screens, or formal
shapes, though its natural habit is also compact. It makes a good,
formal wall tree.
Leaves are dark green
and aromatic; flowers
are small and yellow,
followed by small, dark
berries that are attractive to birds.

The sweet bay requires well-drained
soil but little water
when it is established.
It may need shade in
hot climates. City conditions are tolerated.

Lavandula
angustifolia
(English Lavender)

Perennial
Zones 6–10

English lavender has
been cultivated for
centuries as an ornamental herb and for its
aromatic oil. Recently,
dwarf varieties have
been developed that
are attractive as
ground covers while retaining their fra-

grance. These varieties
all have lance-shaped,
green-gray leaves,
small blue-to-purple
flowers in spikes on
long stems from 8
inches to 2 feet tall,
and a moderate growth
rate. They grow in
clumps 1–2 feet wide
and bloom for about
two months in summer.

English lavender
needs only full sun and
average but well-
drained soil to thrive.
Watering and fertilizing needs are minimal.
Established plants can
be sheared in early
spring to induce dense
growth, but after three
or four years plants get
leggy, and the best
thing to do is to take
them out and replant.

Leptospermum
scoparium
(New Zealand Tea
Tree)

Narrow-leafed evergreen shrub
Zones 9 and 10

For an outstanding floral display from late
winter to spring and
an interesting accent
of finely textured, fragrant evergreen foliage, the New Zealand
tea tree can be an effective choice in gardens with a mild climate, particularly the
Mediterranean cli-

mates of the West
Coast. It is also an excellent choice in seacoast gardens as a
specimen, accent, or focal point in a shrub
border. A wide range of
cultivars is available
for flower color (in
reds, pinks, and white)
and habit (6–10 feet
high to prostrate
ground covers 8–12
inches high and 2–3
feet wide). The prostrate forms make interesting and colorful
ground covers, but
their fairly open habit
permits weeds. Flowers
are profuse and colorful, appearing from
late winter to midsummer.

Leptospermum scoparium must have excellent drainage and
prefers a location in
full sun. Once established, it is drought-
tolerant and pest-free.

Liatris spicata
(Blazing Star,
Gayfeather)

Perennial
Zones 3–10

Tall rose, lavender, or
purple flower spikes
make the blazing star
a useful vertical accent
for the garden. Use it
either singly in a
mixed border or in
groups of three or
more. The individual
flowers resemble tiny
thistle blooms, packed

Liatris spicata

Ligustrum japonicum

Liquidambar styraciflua

Liriope muscari

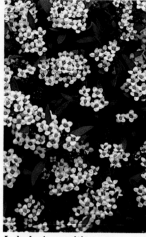

Lobularia maritima

densely along the upper half of the stems. Blooming from July to September, they open over time from the top of the spike to the bottom. Leaves are dark green, almost grasslike, and stemless.

This species responds to moist, well-drained soil high in organic matter and of moderate fertility. It needs abundant water. Give it full sun. It has few pests, but in areas where the southern root-knot nematode is known to be a problem, the plant should be avoided. The plant is long-lived and often self-sows, but it is seldom invasive. Clumps expand slowly by sending up new stems about the base.

Ligustrum species
(Privet)

Evergreen shrub (some deciduous)
Zones 4–10

Privets are highly adaptable and low in maintenance. They are most often used as for- mal and informal hedges, backgrounds, and screens. Most have white, spikelike clusters of strongly scented flowers in early summer, whose scent is variously described as offensive to pleasant.

All privets transplant easily bare root, are adaptable to nearly any soil except a wet one, and take full sun to partial shade. They perform well under adverse conditions of pollution and drought and are pest-free. If flowers are desired, prune just after blooming. All privets are rapidly growing shrubs that respond well to pruning and shaping.

Liquidambar styraciflua
(American Sweet Gum)

Deciduous tree
Zones 2–12

The American sweet gum is one of the most reliable trees for autumn color and a good skyline tree, growing symmetrically to heights of 60 feet or more and widths of 20–25 feet. Its star-shaped leaves, which somewhat resemble maple leaves, turn rich shades of crimson to purple in the fall, the color lasting as long as six weeks. Fruits, which mature in the fall, are the size of golf balls and prickly like burrs. Corky ridges on the branches add winter interest.

The American sweet gum will grow on a wide variety of sites but does best in rich clay or loam soils. It is subject to chlorosis (yellowing of leaves) in heavy alkaline soils; the condition can be contained by adding iron sulfate or chelates. Water requirements vary depending on whether the soil is heavy or sandy. Raking up the fruit is a spring chore.

Liriope species
(Lilyturf)

Evergreen perennial
Zones 5–10

Liriope is characterized by clumps of coarse, mostly dark-green, grasslike leaves up to 2 feet long and less than an inch wide. It and ophiopogon, with which it is sometimes confused, are both members of the lily family, but the liriope is the hardier of the two. 'Big Blue' lilyturf (*Liriope muscari*) gets its name from its 4–8-inch-long, spike-like clusters of flowers that are, in fact, more violet than blue. They appear among the leaves from about July into September, followed by a few blue-black berries. This lilyturf grows rather slowly to a height of 2 feet. It is sometimes listed as *Ophiopogon jaburan*. Creeping lily-turf (*L. spicata*), is smaller in all aspects, forms a dense cover that spreads by underground stems, has pale lavender flowers, and grows at a moderate rate up to a foot high.

L. muscari and *L. spicata* have no special soil or light requirements but are probably grown most often in partial shade, if only for reasons of landscape design. They need only light summer watering. Both are easily propagated by divison. In extremely cold weather leaves turn yellow and should be clipped off before new growth starts in spring.

Lobularia maritima
(Sweet Alyssum)

Annual
All zones

Sweet alyssum (*Lobularia maritima*) is a common late fall (in mild climates) or early spring bedding plant not usually considered a ground cover. It is often used with a new ground cover planting to cover and protect the bare soil while the planting is being established but also works as edging, bulb cover, filler, and in containers. It's very low growing (rarely more than a foot) and has narrow, gray-green leaves. Fragrant,

Nandina domestica

Narcissus 'Ceylon'

quarter-size flowers varying between dark purple and white appear in clusters all season long.

In mild areas, treat sweet alyssum as a short-lived perennial and spread seed or set out small plants as needed. In cold climates, plant in early spring for summer bloom. Full sun (some shade is okay), average soil, and normal watering are all they need to thrive.

Lysimachia nummularia
(Moneywort, Creeping Jenny)

Perennial, used as a ground cover
Zones 3–8

Moneywort is a rapidly spreading creeper that is a weed where you don't want it, as in a lawn, and a ground cover where you do. A natural spot for moneywort is one where there are rocks for it to creep over, as around a small garden pool. The leaves are abundant enough to form a wavy carpet a few inches high. Bright-yellow flowers about three-fourths inch in diameter bloom through the summer.

Moneywort will grow almost anyplace, in sun or shade, provided the soil is moist to wet; and it is a good plant to use where grass won't grow.

Miscanthus sinensis
(Eulalia Grass)

Perennial ornamental grass
Zones 5–8

Large, striking, upright, and gracefully arching at the top, eulalia grass forms dense clumps 6–12 feet tall. The foliage is medium-fine in texture, turning a rich gold that is effective through the winter. The flowers, with their pinkish or silvery 7–10-inch plumes, are also attractive from fall into winter. 'Gracillimus' is a finely textured cultivar with narrow, somewhat curly leaves. 'Variegatus' and 'Zebrinus' have foliage and stems in combinations of green with yellow or white. These cultivars are smaller than the species, rarely exceeding 6 or 7 feet in height.

Eulalia grass performs well in any soil and should have full sun.

Myrica pensylvanica
(Northern Bayberry)

Deciduous shrub
Zones 2–7

Bayberry is excellent for large-scale massing in poor soil and coastal areas and adapts well to difficult urban sites, where it forms rolling, billowing masses of clean, deep, lustrous-green foliage, ranging 5–12 feet in height. It tends to sucker and form large colonies but is also good as a shrub border, informal hedge, and to combine with broad-leafed evergreens. The fruits are grayish white, waxy berries that are produced in great quantities along the stems of female plants and persist all winter long. All parts of the plant are aromatic—the berries have been used since Colonial times to make candles.

Bayberry fixes its own nitrogen from the atmosphere and actually prefers infertile, dry, sandy soils. Transplant from a container into any soil, from sand to clay, and give it full sun to partial shade. It is tolerant of salt spray and wind and attracts no serious pests. Older, leggy plants can be renewed by pruning them down to the ground.

Nandina domestica
(Nandina, Heavenly Bamboo)

Broad-leafed evergreen (semideciduous in the North)
Zones 6B–10

Nandina is popular for its variety of ornamental assets and easy care. A strongly vertical form contrasts nicely with delicate, wispy foliage that is evergreen in mild climates. Erect, creamy-white flower spikes borne on the ends of the vertical branches in June are followed by bright-red clusters of berries. With only a few hours of daily sun, nandina frequently has brilliant crimson-to-purple foliage in the fall and winter. Often reaching 8 feet in height and 2½–3 feet in width, nandina is effective as a hedge or screen, in a mass or grouping, and as a solitary specimen in an entryway or container. It is particularly effective when backlit. In the northern limits of its range, it is best used as a herbaceous perennial.

Nandina performs well in nearly any soil, although it is best in rich soil with plenty of water. Either sun or shade is acceptable (as long as some protection is given in hot climates). Established plants tolerate drought well.

Narcissus species
(Daffodil, Jonquil, Narcissus)

Bulb
Zones 5–9

Without doubt daffodils, jonquils, narcissus, or whatever name you choose to call them (the genus is vast) are the world's favorite bulb. By any name these cheerful, often fragrant, flowers play important roles in the landscape, container gardens indoors and out, and bouquets. Cut narcissus when the flowers are almost fully opened. They will stay fresh for a week.

Plant all narcissus in full sun or partial shade as soon as they are available in early fall. Apply bone meal. Narcissus are the best of the large-flowered bulbs for naturalizing.

Nerium oleander

Nyssa sylvatica

Pachysandra terminalis 'Variegata'

Pelargonium hybrid

Nerium oleander
(Oleander)

Broad-leafed evergreen shrub
Zones 8–10

Oleander is a commonly used shrub in the South and west of the Rockies because of its coarse, evergreen foliage; attractive red, pink, white, or yellow flowers in the summer; and easy care, especially in hot, dry climates. A broad, rounded, and bulky shrub, oleander grows very rapidly to 8–12 feet tall and 6–10 feet wide, sometimes becoming open and leggy. It makes a good hedge or screen and can be trained as a "standard" (single trunk).

Plant oleander in full sun, in any soil from dry sand to wet clay. Heat-, salt-, and drought-tolerant, it is an excellent choice for desert gardens. Prune the shrub in early spring to control size and form. Remove old wood that has flowered each year. Pinch tips to encourage density or pull off suckers from the base to encourage more height. Oleander is plagued by many insects and diseases, particularly in shady or humid environments. Mildew, scale, and aphids are among the most severe.

All parts of the plant are violently poisonous to humans and animals. Be extremely cautious with clippings from pruning. Smoke from burning plant parts, green or dried, can cause severe skin and respiratory irritations. Contact with leaves can give some people dermatitis, and ingesting small amounts can cause severe illness, even death.

Nyssa sylvatica
(Sour Gum)

Deciduous tree
Zones 2–10

Sour gum is a slow-growing tree good for lawns and fall color. Leaves are dark green and glossy, turning to scarlet in the fall. Flowers are inconspicuous. The sour gum reaches heights of 30–50 feet and widths of 15–25 feet; in maturity its habit is spreading and irregular.

The sour gum is easy to maintain. It grows well in almost any soil, can manage poor drainage, is tolerant of a variable water supply, and can withstand occasional drought.

Ophiopogon japonicus
(Mondo Grass)

Perennial
Zones 7–10

Mondo grass is the most grasslike of the lilyturfs. It is identified by dense clumps of long, ⅛-inch-wide leaves that arch over into mounds 8–10 inches high. The leaves are dark green and coarse in texture. Small, pale-purple flowers, mostly hidden among the leaves, appear in July and August; pea-size blue fruit follows. The growth rate is quite slow until the plant is well established.

Mondo grass is adaptable to most well-drained soils. In coastal areas it will grow in full sun; elsewhere it looks and grows best in partial shade. Regular summer watering is a must, with more frequent watering needed if the plant is exposed to full sun in a mass planting.

Osmanthus fragrans
(Sweet Olive)

Broad-leafed evergreen shrub
Zones 8–10

Sweet olive is a compact, neat plant with glossy evergreen foliage that makes an outstanding hedge, screen, background, espalier, or container plant. It is very easy to care for and quite adaptable. The nearly year-round, tiny, white flowers have a powerful sweet scent.

Plant sweet olive in any soil, from sand to clay, and give it partial shade, and it will grow at a moderate rate to a 10-foot-high by 10-foot-wide shrub with a rounded outline. It can easily be kept lower, however, and responds well to shearing. Prune any time of the year; pinch the growing tips to encourage denseness.

Ostrya virginiana
(American Hop Hornbeam)

Deciduous tree
Zones 4–9

The American hop hornbeam is a slow-growing, small, round-headed tree reaching heights of 30–35 feet. Its foliage is dull green, usually with a reddish fall color. The bark of the trunk and larger branches is platelike and sheddy.

This tree is somewhat difficult to transplant, but it tolerates a wide range of soil types. It does well in inner-city conditions.

Pachysandra terminalis
(Japanese Spurge)

Evergreen perennial, used as a ground cover
Zones 4–10

Japanese spurge is widely used throughout the world as a ground cover for shady locations. It's hardy to −30 degrees Fahrenheit and remains evergreen in the most severe winters. Veined, dark-green, oval leaves, 1½–4 inches long and lightly toothed along their up-

Petunia grandiflora 'Ultra Pink'

Pinus mugo var mugo

per half, grow in clusters at the top of upright stems 6–8 inches high. The plant produces white, fragrant flowers and white fruit. It spreads rapidly by underground runners to form a dense cover of essentially uniform height. It is the perfect ground cover to use as a large-scale planting under trees or, on a small scale, in the shade of evergreen shrubs. The variety 'Green Carpet' is a darker green, more flowering form.

Japanese spurge grows only in filtered to full shade and performs best in rich, somewhat moist, acidic soil. New plants can be started by division or rooted cuttings set out 6–12 inches apart in spring. They should be fed during the growing season to heighten color.

Pelargonium × hortorum
(Geranium)

Tender perennial, grown as an annual
All zones

At one time or another, nearly every home gardener has grown geraniums. Easy and vigorous, the geranium is one of the most highly bred and readily available of all annuals.

Philadelphus coronarius

Flowers are intensely colored (and nonfading in some of the newer cultivars) and produced freely over a long season from late spring to frost. In the mildest parts of California and Florida, geraniums are grown as perennials for year-round bloom, sometimes trained to climb up fences or arbors, or planted to spill down steep banks. In harsher climates, year-round color is still possible if you bring the plants indoors for the winter; in fact, geraniums are almost as popular for house plants as for beds and borders.

Geraniums prefer rich, moist, well-drained soil high in organic matter and seem to like slightly acid soil. Full sun is best. Newer cultivars tolerate heat (as well as resist disease) but can be knocked out by prolonged high heat and humidity. Groom geraniums regularly for appearance and to encourage more blooms. Cuttings can be used to start new plants.

Petunia × hybrida
(Petunia)

Annual
All zones

The petunia is the most popular annual in the United States. Its many varieties are dependable and versatile, and their season is long. Leaves are thick and broad, and flowers are fragrant, in many colors.

Petunias are one of the few annuals whose young seedlings can withstand a full, hot sun. Well-drained, light sandy soil is best. Shade discourages flowering. Varieties with single blossoms will tolerate heavier, more alkaline soils. Water moderately and feed liberally, at least once a month. In containers allow to dry out between waterings. Pinch or shear plants twice: once when 6 inches tall and again after the first wave of flowers. This will promote density and full flowering.

Philadelphus coronarius
(Sweet Mock Orange)

Deciduous shrub
Zones 5–8

The white, May flowers of the sweet mock orange are legendary for their powerful fragrance and have been popular for ages. Mock orange grows rapidly to an upright and irregular height and width of 10–12 feet. Use sweet mock orange where its fragrance can be appreciated–in a border, near outdoor living areas, entryways, and windows. Since mock orange varieties vary in fragrance, it is safest to select for fragrance only when the plants are in flower.

Mock orange is easy to grow, not particular about soil, and will perform well in sun or partial shade. Free from serious pests, its wide-ranging root system is highly competitive and indicative of its tolerance to adverse conditions. It requires annual pruning to maintain a semblance of presentability. Do so right after it completes flowering by removing all older wood or cutting it to the ground. ground.

Pinus mugo var. mugo
(Dwarf Mugo Pine)

Conifer
Zones 2–8 (but not in the desert)

Dwarf mugo pine is often sold as a diminutive, cute little cushion that will grow only 2–4 feet high. Beware. Many homeowners are surprised to find a 10-by-15-foot haystack monster on their doorsteps fifteen or so years later. If a reliably small plant is desired, seek out the harder-to-find cultivars, such as 'Compacta', 'Gnome', or 'Slavinii'. Use the mugo pine for textural evergreen interest in a foundation planting, as low masses, or in groupings.

Plant the mugo pine in moist, deep loam in full sun or partial shade. It requires little fertilizing and is fairly drought-tolerant, though it suffers in conditions of air pollution. Good drainage is important. To maintain a compact, dense form, the mugo pine can be pruned annually in spring by removing approximately two-thirds of each young candle.

Pittosporum tobira

Platanus × acerifolia

Pyrus calleryana

Portulaca grandiflora

Pittosporum tobira
(Japanese Pittisporum)

Evergreen shrub
Zones 9 and 10

Pittosporum tobira is a shrub or small tree 6–15 feet or more high. The variety 'Wheeler's Dwarf' grows to about 2 feet and is very useful as a ground cover for certain applications. It has a mounding growth habit and a moderate growth rate. *P. tobira* has thick, leathery leaves, roughly oval in shape and ¾–1½ inches long. They are dark green, densely set along the branches, most heavily at the tips. Orange-scented white flowers that become cream colored with age appear in dense clusters at the branch tips in spring.

This is a sturdy plant that grows well in most soils in full sun or partial shade. Water regularly and feed at least once a year. Watch for aphids and scale insects. Keep pruning to a minimum.

Platanus × acerifolia
(London Plane Tree)

Deciduous tree
Zones 5–9

The London plane tree is a fast-growing, versatile, widely adapted tree, frequently used as a street or mall tree. It attains heights of 40–60 feet. Leaves are bright green and large lobed, and they do not change color in fall. Fruits are brown and ball shaped, borne two to a cluster. The most attractive feature of this tree is its striking green and white flaking bark.

Water thoroughly and deeply in summer and watch for blight, which causes unnatural leaf drop.

Portulaca grandiflora
(Rose Moss)

Annual
All zones

Rose moss forms loose, trailing mats of brittle stems and tiny, fleshy leaves covered with brilliantly colored flowers in many shades. The petals have a distinctive sheen, like watered silk. Many varieties have double or ruffled flowers. The flowers close late in the day and during cloudy weather, which diminishes their use in climates of frequent haze or clouds. Rose moss makes an excellent ground cover for sunny, dry banks and areas of poor soil. It reaches its height of beauty scattered in small patches throughout the rock garden or between paving stones.

Rose moss thrives in situations inimical to most annuals. Intense heat, a dry, rocky soil, even nearly pure sand are all conditions that it loves. Good drainage and full sun are necessary. It withstands heat and drought well. Water infrequently. Avoid overwatering. Rose moss reseeds readily, so once you plant it, expect it to be around for a while.

Pyrus calleryana
(Callery Pear)

Deciduous tree
Zones 2–10

The species has many good qualities: abundant spring bloom, brilliant crimson-red fall color, shiny dark-green leaves with scalloped edges, and amazing adaptability. With the development of cultivars like 'Bradford', which are thornless, fireblight-resistant, and have small fruits of no inconvenience, the Callery pear has become one of the most attractive specimens available. It is also one of the most versatile.

All cultivars stand up to pollution and other stresses of the city and can take wind, even on the coast. They are undemanding with reference to soil type, require little maintenance, and are drought-resistant and relatively free from pests and diseases. Check with your local nursery or garden center for varieties adapted to your area.

Raphiolepis indica
(India Hawthorne)

Broad-leafed evergreen shrub
Zones 8B–10

India hawthorne is one of those easy-to-care-for garden workhorses that is both spectacularly showy and extremely serviceable for a multitude of purposes. Its leathery, evergreen foliage and neat, dense, restrained habit, 3–5 feet high and wide, make it an excellent low background, mass, informal hedge, or large-scale ground cover. Consider it as a foreground or facing plant in a shrub border, or as an excellent, troublefree container plant. The flowers bloom in midwinter or spring, usually repeating in the fall, and vary from white to red, according to the cultivar.

India hawthorne prefers full sun but tolerates partial shade well, in addition to a variety of soils. While reasonably tolerant of drought,

Rhododendron 'Brazil'

it looks its best when frequently watered. Minimize splashing water onto foliage, since fireblight and leaf spots can be problems; and protect from aphids.

Rhododendron species
(Rhododendrons and Azaleas)

Some evergreen, some deciduous species
Zones 2–10

Probably no other group of plants elicits as much devotional praise and obsessional frustration as the genus *Rhododendron*. Where they can be grown, few plants can match the bewildering variety of striking, often brilliant flowers borne in legendary profusion. Besides their famous flowers, rhododendrons and azaleas frequently offer outstanding form and foliage, along with more subtle qualities apparent on close inspection.

If planted in a favorable location and given the proper growing conditions, azaleas and rhododendrons are easy, care-free, and long-living plants. Rhododendrons need well-drained, moisture-retaining, acid soil; protection from winter sun and wind and excessive heat; and adequate atmospheric and soil moisture. Do not overfeed. Pruning is seldom necessary.

Rhus copallina

Rhus copallina
(Flameleaf Sumac, Shining Sumac)

Deciduous shrub
Zones 5–8

Flameleaf sumac is the best sumac for ornamental use, although nurseries seldom offer it, preferring its larger, weedier, and shorter-lived cousin, the staghorn sumac. While occasionally reaching 30 feet in the wild, this open, picturesque shrub rarely exceeds 8 feet in cultivation. It will spread into clumps through suckering, but in a much more restrained and controllable manner than the staghorn sumac. Its shiny-green foliage is darker than any other sumac, and the compound, large, almost tropical leaves turn a brilliant red-orange in the fall. Unlike other sumacs, the flameleaf sumac is an excellent subject for containers; or use it as a specimen for fall color and interesting silhouettes. It is also beautiful when naturalized in large groups and masses.

Flameleaf sumac is easily transplanted and adaptable to many soils but prefers well-drained ones, being intolerant of standing water.

Rosmarinus officinalis
(Dwarf Rosemary)

Evergreen shrub
Zones 8–10

Dwarf rosemary is a woody evergreen, well known in its taller form for its various herbal uses. The creeping variety *Rosmarinus officinalis* 'Prostratus' grows slowly along the ground, spreading 4–8 feet. Normal height is about 8 inches but in a mass planting can be expected to mound up to 2 feet, particularly as plants mature. It has the typically aromatic, narrow, deep-green leaves and tiny clusters of light-blue, half-inch flowers that bloom the greater part

Rosmarinus officinalis 'Lockwood de Forest'

Rudbeckia (hybrid double) and *Echinops* 'Taplow Blue'

of the year, most heavily in winter and spring.

This plant grows well in almost any soil as long as it has good drainage; it will not tolerate soggy soil. Rosemary is drought-tolerant but grows best with some additional water in very dry areas. Little or no fertilizer is needed. Propagate by seed or by cuttings. Plants get woody as they get older; control and rejuvenate by cutting out dead wood.

Rudbeckia hirta var. *pulcherrima* 'Gloriosa Daisy'
(Gloriosa Daisy, Brown-eyed Susan)

Perennial, often treated as an annual
All zones

Most of the many species of rudbeckia are perennial. All are robust and vigorous. Gloriosa daisies are actually short-lived perennials, treated as annuals, that bloom well the first year from seed, if planted early enough. They are rugged flowers with foliage to match and look best in rows or groups behind shorter flowers that can hide their rough leaves. Many varieties are available, with single or double flowers in solid and bicolored yellow, gold, orange, and bronze, all with chocolate brown centers. Handsome in the rear of a border, they also make stunning beds all to themselves. The flowers are long lasting when cut.

The gloriosa daisy does best in rich, moist, well-drained soil high in organic matter, but it will tolerate poor, dry soil. Flowering is abundant in intense summer heat.

Salvia splendens 'Blaze of Fire'

Sempervivum tectorum

Spirea vanhouttii

Salvia splendens
(Scarlet Sage)

Annual
All zones

Salvia splendens is one of the most popular spike-flowered annuals for large-scale bedding and bright color, especially in parks and other public places. It provides some of the brightest, most intense reds and scarlets known to the gardener. *S. farinacea* (blue sage), although lesser known, is an equally useful plant. As its more subtle colors are apt to get lost when mixed in a border, its most stunning effect is achieved by massing it in great background sheets. The foliage is nicely grayish, which complements the flower color. In warmer climates it will act as a perennial from year to year. Both of these sages are long lasting when cut for vases.

S. splendens and *S. farinacea* perform admirably with a minimum of attention. Neither is fussy about soil.

Sedum species
(Stonecrop)

Perennial
Zones 3–10

There are more than 300 species and at least twice as many varieties of sedum. There are tiny sedums forming mats only 1 or 2 inches high and others that reach 2 feet. A few flower abundantly; others are shy bloomers. The beauty of the plants is in the shape and color of their leaves. They are, by definition, rock plants, although their use is by no means confined to rock gardens. There are species effective on slopes, between stepping-stones, as a mass planting, as container plants, and, especially, blended with other ground covers such as the prostrate junipers.

Sedums root easily from cuttings; they even propagate themselves from broken leaves. Sedums are not particular about soil or water. As a guide, use the least amount of water that will keep them healthy and colorful. There are no serious pest problems.

Sempervivum tectorum
(Hen-and-Chickens)

Succulent
Zones 5–10

Hen-and-chickens is a plant well known to American gardeners, having arrived with the earliest settlers. Leaves are fleshy and grow in rosettes. The flowers are red and grow on stems up to 2 feet tall. Planted around rocks, hen-and-chickens will quickly fill in cracks and crevices. On dry slopes it can outgrow most weeds. In medieval years, these plants were used for binding soil on the sod roofs of cottages (the species name *tectorum* is a Latin word meaning "roof"). Many different selections and varieties possess different colors and heights.

Watering is not usually necessary except during unusually long droughts. In a good soil, growth will be faster. Propagate by separating offsets.

Soleirolia soleirolii
(Baby's-Tears)

Perennial, used as a ground cover.
Zones 9 and 10

Baby's-tears is a creeping, mosslike plant that forms a dense, soft carpet 1–3 inches high. The foliage is composed of tiny, light-green, rounded leaves growing in a tight mat. These plants provide a cool, delicate effect when used at the base of trees or shade plants like ferns, camellias, and azaleas. The plant is well named for it is as fragile as a baby's tear. A few steps will not kill it, but the footprints will remain for days.

Baby's-tears needs shade, rich soil, and moisture. It is quickly killed by direct sun, drought, or subfreezing temperatures.

Spiraea species
(Spirea)

Deciduous shrub
Zones 5–10

To most, the word *spirea* means bridle-wreath or Vanhoutte spirea, two old-fashioned favorites. Many superior, dwarfed varieties are available to the diligent searcher. Flower colors range from red to rose to white. The branches are arching and fountainlike, a stunning sight when in flower. Use spireas in a shrub border as an inexpensive, rapidly growing, and easy-care filler.

Easily transplanted, fast growing, and low in maintenance, spireas are not particular about soil. They are subject to many pests, including fireblight, leaf spot, powdery mildew, and a host of insects, but none appears to be fatal if the plants are placed in a location with full sun and good air circulation. Spireas differ in pruning requirements. Summer-flowering types should be pruned in late winter or early spring, since they bloom on the current year's wood; spring-flowering types should be pruned directly after blooming. Older, leggy plants of either type can be renewed by cutting them to the ground in early spring.

Tagetes 'Glowing Embers'

Tagetes erecta
(African Marigold)

Tagetes erecta × *T. patula*
(Triploid or 3-N Marigold)

Tagetes patula
(French Marigold)

Annuals
All zones

Brilliant, easy color is the hallmark of the marigold, and the immense popularity of this cheerful plant has led to extensive hybridizing, resulting in an array of forms that can be confusing. Foliage is fernlike, usually quite aromatic. All bear either single or double flowers in the familiar yellows, golds, and oranges, some bicolored with red or brown stripes.

Healthy marigolds are easy to grow. They are rugged and tough and require only the minimum of attention. Adequate water and full sun are necessary, but too much water will cause root rot. Too much fertilizer creates foliage disproportionate to flowers. Taller plants need staking for protection from wind and rain, but the shorter varieties are more resistant to foul-weather damage than any other annuals. Marigolds self-sow profusely, and the new progeny will be full of surprises, as this plant—especially hybrid forms—is variable from seed.

Taxus baccata

Taxus species
(Yew)

Conifer
Zones 5, 6B–8

While the species are large, 40–50-foot-high trees, the many cultivars available are among the most useful coniferous evergreen shrubs for the landscape. Hardy and trouble-free, with handsome dark-green foliage and a wide variety of dense, refined forms, about the only drawback they have is overuse. Like junipers, yews are often planted without consideration for their ultimate size. Your nursery will help you to select the appropriate variety, but be sure to ask how big it will grow. Yews accept formal pruning well and are often clipped into hedges or other shapes. Consider them also for massing, as an evergreen touch to a shrub border, and as a foundation plant. When allowed to develop their natural forms, the effect is usually graceful and appealing.

Give yews soil with excellent drainage, and they will prove to be generally easy to grow and pest-free, in sun or shade. In heavy, wet soils they will be stunted and sickly, if they survive at all. Give them adequate moisture and protect them from sweeping wind. In hot, dry climates, give them a northern exposure and hose the foliage frequently during the driest periods. Beware of their colorful, red fruits, the inner portions of which are poisonous.

Thuja occidentalis
(American Arbovitae)

Conifer
Zones 2–10

While *Thuja occidentalis* is naturally a large, upright, coniferous tree growing 40–60 feet tall, many slow-growing cultivars are available and often used in foundation plantings, as hedges, or as screens. Varieties range from inches-high, rock garden plants to 20-foot, columnar small trees that are useful as screens. Scalelike leaves in sprays are bright green ranging to yellow.

Thuja occidentalis 'Globosa Rhindiana'

Tropaeolum majus

Most cultivars turn yellow-brown in cold weather—'Nigra' and 'Techny' retain dark-green foliage all winter long.

Plant American arbovitae in well-drained, moist soil in full sun. It is tolerant of highly alkaline soils and performs best in areas of high atmospheric moisture. The branches and foliage are quite susceptible to damage from winter winds, snow, and ice. While many pests are potential problems, these trees are generally easy to care for and trouble-free.

Tropaeolum majus
(Nasturtium)

Annual
All zones

Nasturtiums thrive in the poorest soils and require little care if grown in the right spot. Many colors and bicolors of nasturtium are available, and these named hybrids are superior to the usual orange type. Some are dense, compact, bushy plants, growing only 12 inches high and maybe twice as wide. Some are semi-trailing types and will creep around in a 2–6 foot circle. Others are trailing plants or weak climbers that may reach 6–10 feet in length. All bear the characteristically round-shaped, sharp-tasting nasturtium leaf.

Give nasturtiums the coolest spot in the garden. They grow best in sandy, dry, and infertile but well-drained soil. Avoid overwatering and feeding with high-nitrogen fertilizer. If soil is too rich, there will be much foliage and few flowers. Nasturtiums tolerate drought.

Viburnum dilatatum

Xylosma congestum

Viburnum species
(Viburnum)

Evergreen or deciduous shrub
Zones 3–10

Viburnum is a particularly diverse genus that contains a wide range of valuable shrubs for the garden. Some are grown for their moderately attractive and powerfully fragrant blossoms; others display extremely showy combinations of flower, fruit, and fall color.

Most viburnums are widely adaptable to variations in climate. They perform best in a moist, well-drained soil that is slightly acid, although they are generally quite adaptable to other soils. Either sun or shade is fine. Prune or shear according to the type. Many insects and diseases can attack viburnums, although these shrubs are usually untroubled if kept vigorous.

Vinca major, Vinca minor
(Periwinkle)

Evergreen perennial used as a ground cover
Zones 4–10

In form, structure, and growth habit, the periwinkles, *Vinca major* and *Vinca minor,* are the same. The main differences are that *V. major* is coarser than *V. minor,* grows three to four times as high, is strongly invasive,

Vinca major

and less hardy. Both are evergreen trailers. They spread rapidly, the stems rooting as they trail. The leaves are a glossy dark green, growing oppositely about every inch or so along the stems. In the spring, lilac-blue flowers appear in moderate numbers toward the ends of the stems. *V. minor* is among the best of the evergreen ground covers, not only because of its hardiness but also because of its quiet, cool beauty. It is an excellent choice for medium-scale planting, particularly in the filtered shade of large trees or shrubs. It is also effective in raised beds or planters where it might trail for several feet over a wall. *V. major* is useful as a large-scale ground cover on a slope, particularly in naturalistic gardens.

These plants grow best in light shade and a good, moist, well-drained soil. They can be propagated by divi-

sion or from stem or root cuttings. *V. minor* grows in any climate in the country with the exception of hot desert areas.

Xylosma congestum
(Shiny Xylosma)

Broad-leafed evergreen
Zones 8–10

Valued for its clean, shiny, yellow-green foliage in all seasons, shiny xylosma will slowly grow in height and width to 8–10 feet, a rounded, loose shrub or small tree. Xylosma responds well to pruning and can easily be trained into an espalier. It can also be used in a shrub border or foundation planting, as a container plant, as a formal or informal hedge, or for a high bank or ground cover. Some forms are spiny and make useful barriers.

Plant xylosma in any soil. It tolerates heat and drought but looks best when it has adequate water.

Zinnia elegans 'Miss'

Zinnia angustifolia
(Narrowleaf Zinnia)

Zinnia elegans
(Common Zinnia)

Zinnia haageana
(Mexican Zinnia)

Annuals
All zones

The hundreds of zinnia cultivars are usually grouped into three categories according to size—dwarf, intermediate, and tall—but the lines are not distinct. Within each category many strains of flower form and size have been developed, in nearly every color of the rainbow. The dwarf and intermediate varieties are excellent for bedding or containers, as they flower abundantly and often spread quite wide. Use

the taller varieties toward the rear of a mixed border and in the cutting garden, where any necessary staking will be least noticeable.

Zinnias are easy to grow. Give them plenty of heat and air circulation, and avoid cool locations of damp, stagnant air. Never water late in the day, and carefully avoid getting any moisture on the foliage. It is best to soak or flood when watering, but be sure to water regularly. Mildew can be a severe problem; use fungicide if it appears. Fertilize regularly. Pinching young plants will result in denser foliage and more blooms. Remove spent blossoms.

Index